A COURSE FOR ELEMENTARY ENGLISH TEACHER EDUCATION

A practical guide to teaching English to children in English

JAEHYUK KIM, YOUNGSUK KIM, KYUSOO SUN,
MARIA OH, SEONHO PARK

INTELLIGENCE COMMUNITY

A COURSE FOR ELEMENTARY ENGLISH TEACHER EDUCATION:
A practical guide to teaching English to children in English

INTELLIGENCE COMMUNITY
5-16 Munhwajeondang- ro 23, Dong-gu,
Gwangju, Korea

First published 2005
Second impression 2006
Fourth impression 2008
Fifth impression 2011
Sixth impression 2012
Seventh impression 2014
5th impression 2022
6th impression 2024

ISBN : 978-89-6103-269-8 93370

Authors' acknowledgements
For our students and colleagues at the Universities of Education
in Korea and the members of the program development project

Contents

To the Student

The book, ***A Course for Elementary English Teacher Education: A practical guide to teaching English to children in English*** is a teacher-training program based on the principle ***Teach English in English.*** This book has been supported by the Ministry of Education (Research Number: 2004-9-9) as part of a project to guide Korea's national universities of education in developing standardized courses for elementary teacher education.

In addition, this book has been written in English to provide a practical teacher-training program for prospective elementary English teachers, who need to develop their English teaching skills and improve their English language skills.

Throughout this book, which contains seventeen chapters, the goal is for prospective elementary English teachers to learn and practice English teaching theories and skills applicable to young learners. Each chapter contains many types of exercises, which serve to connect teaching theories and skills to classroom application. Moreover, the exercises encourage the use of English in the classroom for oral presentation, discussion, teaching demonstrations, and various reading and writing activities.

While listening to the lectures and doing the activities provided in this book, which uses English as the medium of instruction, readers will quickly realize that they are not only learning how to teach English to children, but also practicing English for real communication.

Chapter 1
First Language Acquisition

Chapter One presents the process of first language (L1) acquisition. The emphasis is on what children know about their first language and how they have acquired it. In this chapter, you will understand how L1 children go through a set of developmental stages in order to master their L1. You should keep in mind that children's language development takes place in a rich learning environment where they are exposed daily to their L1 and they have many chances to speak it. You will apply your understanding of L1 acquisition to teaching English to children in Korea. The tasks included in this chapter offer you the chance to use theory to explain language learning and teaching.

In this chapter, we will consider:
(1) What does "acquiring a language" mean?
(2) When do infants produce their first word? Why?
(3) What are the three main views on language development?
(4) What are the main stages of L1 acquisition?

L1 Acquisition

- Children learn a first language in normal circumstances, whatever the language may be. A Korean child born in Paris will acquire French as easily as a French child does. And the reverse is also true. This L1 learning process begins with the production of recognizable sounds around the age of one. It continues throughout the pre-school period, and by the age of 5, children usually have acquired most of the basic skills of oral language.

◆ **L1:** first language; native language of a person.
◆ **L2:** second language.
◆ **FL:** foreign language.
◆ **Acquire:** get by experience; i.e., pick up a language naturally without direct instruction, as in the way children learn languages through meaningful conversations.

- Acquiring a first language means that the speaker can control these five aspects of the language (also see page 40 in Chapter 3):

  (1) Phonology: the sounds of the language.
  (2) Vocabulary: the words of the language.
  (3) Grammar: the rules about how to put words together to produce sentences in the language. It concerns how to make sentences by combining words.
  (4) Discourse: the rules about how to put sentences together to fulfill some functions, e.g. telling stories, explaining how to use a vacuum cleaner, playing hide-and-seek, starting a lesson. It concerns how to make discourse by combining sentences.
  (5) Socio-linguistics: the rules about how to use the language appropriately, e.g. greeting the teacher vs. greeting classmates, asking one's friend for help vs. asking a stranger for help.

◆ **Phonology:** English children usually acquire about 43 speech sounds, 24 consonants and 19 vowels (see pages 78, 79).

- Similarly Hoff-Ginsberg (1997, p.6) divides language development into

  phonological development (sound and sound patterns),
  lexical development (words),
  syntactic development (sentences and grammar),
  and the development of communicative competence.

- On the whole, vocabulary, phonology and grammar concern knowledge and skills about language, but discourse and socio-linguistics concern the use of language for communication. Simply stated, acquiring a language means the speaker has knowledge about the language and the skills to use it.
- Let us suppose you give your first English lesson to 3rd graders. How will

you start the lesson? What information and the skills do you need? Perhaps you might need:

(1) Expressions for greeting, and introducing yourself, small talk… (discourse).
(2) Expressions understandable to ten-year olds (socio-linguistics).
(3) Correct sentence construction (grammar).
(4) Correct words (vocabulary).
(5) Clear and correct pronunciation (phonology)

- An example could be:

Hi, children. I'm your English teacher. My name is Kim Minsu. You call me Mr. Kim. Say "Hello, Mr. Kim." (Students say it.) Good! (Looking at a student) What's your name? (After hearing her name) Hello, Kisun. It's cold today. I'm wearing a sweater, because it's cold. Are you cold? Let's exercise. Put your hands up. Hands up! Put your hands down. Up. Down. Good!

◆ What does "acquiring a language" mean? It means that the speaker ________________
____
____
____
____

Speech Organs of Infants

- Infants have a great capacity for listening, but their capacity for speaking is limited. Newborn infants cannot control the speech-related organs over which adults have good control. To speak normally, children need the ability:

(1) To control and coordinate the movement of their speech organs (e.g., pharynx, larynx, soft palate, jaw, lips, tongue);
(2) To control and combine the respiratory cycle with the activity of the vocal cords (i.e., vocal folds).

- Figure 1 shows our speech organs. A newborn child does not speak, because he cannot control the organs appropriately. In order to speak, he will have to wait until his speech organs fully develop and become functional. His vocal organs should be ready to produce sounds when he is around one.

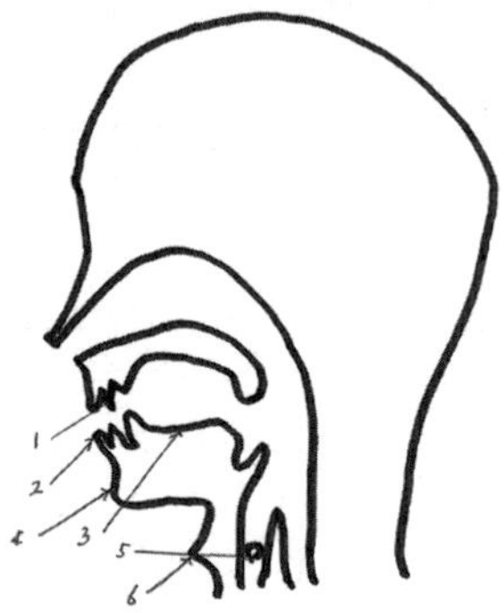

1. teeth 2. lip
3. tongue
4. jaw
5. vocal cords
6. Adam's apple

Figure 1. Speech Organs

- When we say "Hello, nice weather today," we usually use more than 100 muscles. But the organs and muscles of a newborn infant are not physically fit for speech. They develop step by step.
- Hence infants' acquisition of L1 is connected with the development of their vocal organs and muscles. Once they begin to move the muscles to control the larynx, soft palate, jaw, lips, and tongue, they start producing syllables and words.

Views of Language Development

- How do children learn to talk after their speech organs are ready? No one has a complete answer to this question. Scholars have different views on this hot issue as (Hoff-Ginsberg, 1997):

  ① Nature-nurture debate (Is the children's language development the result of circumstances or the result of human nature?),
  ② Language-specific and general cognition debate (Is the language acquisition device language-specific, or not?)
  ③ Functionist-formalist debate (Does language function shape the nature of language acquisition and the form of language or are they irrelevant?)

- Among these debates, the nature-nurture debate has a long history that predates the modern study of language development. In this section, focus is given on the views related to the nature-nurture debate.
- Look at Figure 2. As shown in this figure, children are believed to have the ability to acquire language within their brain. When they receive language input from the environment, language development takes place by using this internal faculty. Some scholars (nativists) emphasize the language learning device, while some others (empirisists) point to the environment where the child is placed.

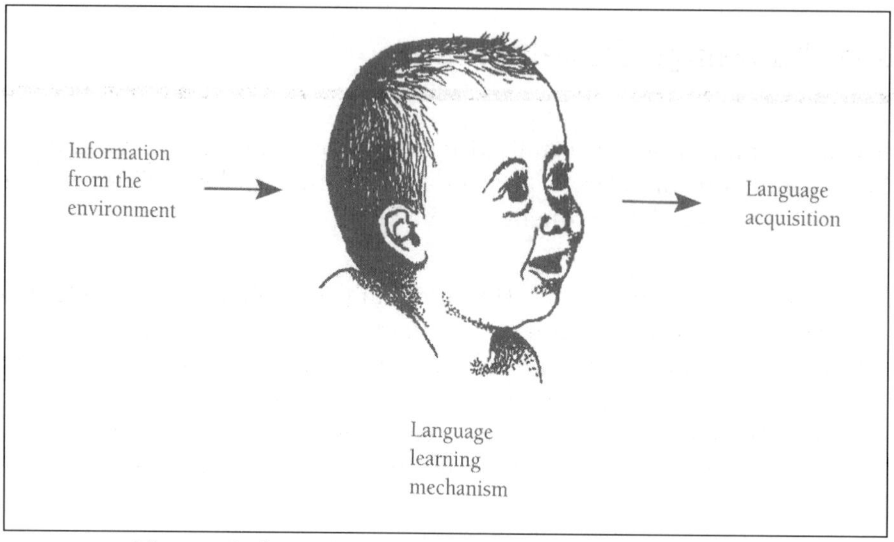

Figure 2. A model of child language development
(Hoff-Ginsberg, 1997)

1. The Nativist View

- Nativists think the language development of a child is the result of human nature (like the ability to sit and walk). They argue that the mind of a child at birth is not a blank slate; rather the child has some innate structure and ability to learn language and knowledge naturally. They believe that children acquire language using this innate ability.
- Nativist scholars point to these three facts as supporting evidence:

  (1) Children acquire language rapidly;
  (2) Children acquire language effortlessly;
  (3) Children acquire language without direct instruction (Hoff-Ginsberg, 1997).

- According this view, language learning is not something that the child does. It is something that happens to the child, much as the child's body grows and matures when provided with appropriate nutrition and environment.

2. The Empiricist View

- Empiricists assert that the mind is at birth like a sheet of blank paper. All knowledge and reason come from experience. Hence, the development of language in children is the result of the circumstances in which children are nurtured. According to this view, children learn language in the same way as they develop table manners or the ability to do calculus.

3. The Interactionist View

- Interacionism is a modern form of empiricism. Scholars of interactionism acknowledge that children have the innate ability to develop language rapidly. However, they argue that interaction with other people plays an important role in language development. In this view, children develop language, not only by using their inborn mental and physical abilities, but also by operating on information provided by the society and environment. Constructivism is another term for this type of position.
- As supporting evidence, interactionists point to the fact that if a child is isolated from human interaction he does not acquire language. The wild boy of Aveyron is good support for this view. In the winter of 1800, a young boy who had been living wild in the woods near Aveyron, France, was found. He was naked. He occasionally ran on all fours. He ate roots, acorns, and raw vegetables. He was able to make sounds, but he had no language. This case shows that humans become what they are as a result of society's influence.

> ◆Constructivism: a philosophy of learning founded on the premise that learners construct their own understanding of the world by reflecting on their experiences. In this theory, learners make and change their own rules and mental models and use them to understand the world.

Stages of L1 Acquisition

- Children develop their L1 stage by stage. These stages are different from each other depending on the child's developmental level. They might be different in terms of phonology, vocabulary, grammar, discourse and/or pragmatics. Look at this data.

At 1 year: Uh-oh (when things fall). At 2 years: Mine ball (my ball). At 2⅔ years: I no want go in there. At 3 years: I wish I could sit on a horse and ride him to every house in the world.

- As shown in the above data, newborn infants, who do not speak or understand any language, become young children who comment, question and express their ideas through language. This change occurs step by step in their phonology, vocabulary, grammar, discourse and pragmatics, over a certain period of time. It is known that children acquire their first language in a sequence, fairly similar to one another, starting from babbling sounds at the age of 5~8 months to producing discourse at the pre-school age. This L1 development of four stages is well known:

1. Pre-Linguistic Stage: 0~12 Months

- This is the period of the infant's language development that extends from birth to the production of his/her first word (Ingram, 1989). At this stage, infants' vocal cords are placed in such a way that they can suck milk from a bottle easily. But because of the unusual location of their vocal cords, they cannot produce words yet.
- **Babbling sounds**: At first, babies' babble includes a wide variety of meaningless sounds, because they do not distinguish human sounds from non-human sounds. Soon they begin to babble human sounds. They imitate the human sounds which they hear in the words of those around them.
- **Babbling syllables**: At the age of 5~8 months, babies start producing syllables like *ba, ma,* and *ga.* These are open syllables (i.e., syllables ending with vowels) and are easy to pronounce. Soon the one-syllable babbling develops into two-syllable babbling like *mama, booboo, and peepee.* At this stage babies are practicing various sounds, and most of these babbling sounds are difficult to understand, even though they have any meaning to them.

2. Single Word Utterance Stage: 12 ~18 Months

- Between 9 and 12 months, many children produce their first word or words. Some children produce their first word earlier than others as seen in this table (Ingram, 1989, p.140).

Table 1. Age of First Word Production

Age of first word production	Number of children
8-9 months	10
10 months	19
12-13 months	10
14-15 months	5
16-17 months	2

- For several months after the appearance of their first words, most children learn words slowly. Smith (1926) and Benedict (1979) examined the average vocabulary size (productive vocabulary) of children at different age periods as seen in Table 2.

Table 2. Average Vocabulary Size of Children

Age (months)	Number of words
7	0
10	1
12	3
15	19
18	50
21	140

- Table 2 shows that the size of a child's vocabulary generally does not grow rapidly at first. During the first several months after speaking their first words, children add an average of 1~6 words to their vocabulary each month (Benedict, 1979). During this period of slow lexical growth, exposure to a new word does not necessarily lead to word learning.
- When children achieve a 50-word vocabulary (around the age of one and half), the rate at which they learn new words changes suddenly; they generally acquire 22~37 words per month. Scholars call this the **word spurt** or the **word explosion**. This spurt occurs for most children around

the age of 18 months.

- Often the first words children speak are tied to particular contexts. For example, Allison produced the word "car" at the age of 9 months only when she was looking at cars on the street from her apartment window. She broadened the meaning of the word as her experience of social interactions increased.
- Children's first words contain names of important people and objects (daddy, cookie) and social words (bye-bye). For a child at this stage, a word represents a number of meanings. For instance, "kitty" may mean from "there is a cat," or "I am scared of the cat," or something else entirely.

> ◆ **Productive vocabulary**: the words the speaker can use in their speech and writing.
> ◆ **Receptive vocabulary**: the words the speaker can understand but can't use in their speech and writing.
> ◆ **Word spurt**: the phenomenon during which children begin to learn and say new words rapidly when they are around 18 months old. It seems that the word spurt has something to do with the growth of the brain.

3. Two Word Utterance Stage: 18~24 Months

- As children acquire more words, they begin combining two or more words to make the meaning of their speech more accurate. This is a gradual process toward producing sentences. In the following are some examples of word combinations (Hoff-Ginsberg, 1997, p.138).

  Possessives: *daddy coffee, daddy hat, Andrew book, daddy tea, Elliot boat*
  Action: *mommy sit, daddy sit, Andrew walk, daddy work*
  Adjectives: *big balloon, big juice, all wet pants, shirt wet, hot tea, boom-boom car, boom-boom plane*

- For some children the two-word stage lasts for several months. For other children, the two-word stage is very brief and it is barely identifiable from the stage of multiword speech. These examples are produced by a 2-year-old child. His English has a lot of content words, but very few function words.

I want some eggs.
I watching cars.
Put it table.
Daddy get you.

- These examples are also from a 2-year old child. They show that the child is using simplified English in terms of pronunciation, word order, and structure.

  Take manana (banana)
  Me not tit (sit)
  Mummy gib (give)
  Baby krip (crib)
  Me lili (little)
  No see guk (duck)
  This not bu (blue)
  No me leep (sleep)
  Eat ola (granola=cereal)
  Allgone ti (twig)

4. Pre-School Period: 24 Months ~ 6 Years

- During the pre-school years, children acquire 6~10 new words (receptive and productive words) a day (Tabors, 1997, p.8). They like to play with words like rhyming and identifying initial sounds in a word. They also like to experiment with combinations of words and to develop grammar. Read these examples and think about how the child develops Yes/No questions.

  Stage 1: See hole? Sit chair? Jamie water?
  Stage2: See my doggie? That black too? I have it?
  You can't fix it?
  Stage3: Does lions walk? Will you help me?
  Can't you work this morning?

- During this period, children begin to produce utterances in which three or more words are combined. A child may speak in sentences which have 10 or more words when he is around the age of 5. He will have mastered the basic sentence structures by that time. The children at this stage are known to add about 600 words (productive words) to their vocabulary a year. They will communicate using 2,000~2,500 words when they are about six.

- At the pre-school stage, children also broaden their understanding of the words they already know by interacting more heavily with their environment. Thus the words they already know take on additional meanings. In addition, they develop the ability to construct discourse through telling stories, making an argument, explaining how to solve a math problem, etc. Furthermore, this is the stage at which children begin to speak pragmatically; for example, using polite and less polite expressions depending on the hearer.

Task 1: Reflect

1. The following words are typically among the first 50 words that children learn to say and use. Classify these words by the types of concepts which they express.

   Ball, allgone, no, dog, give, bye-bye, dirty, cat, baby, go, juice, Mummy, hi, nice, yes, up, stop, shoe, Daddy, milk, car, more, this, down, put, biscuit, sit, clock, key, blanket, sock, sofa, floor, lamp, nappy, pants, house, tree, park

   (1) Naming things or people: ____________________

   (2) Actions/events: ____________________

   (3) Describing/modifying things: ____________________

   (4) Personal/social words: ____________________

◆ We can find from the data that the first words of children belong to four main types. They are ____________________

2. Read the data from two children of different ages (Peccei, 1994). Analyze the data, paying attention to their L1 stages of development. Use the guide below.

- Underline the mistakes the child made.
- What does the mother do about the mistakes?
- What does the mother do to make the conversations continue?

Age: 2; C: child, M: mother

C: me want that.
M: what is it?
C: seen.
M: plasticine?
C: mmmm
C: you take a bissy.
M: 'cause I was hungry.
C: me want a bissy.
C: (later) you put bissy on there.
M: I didn't put biscuit on there.
C: (later) me want neither bissy.

C: me want that pano.
M: you've got a real piano.
C: why?
M: it's upstairs.
C: why? Why?
M: what do you mean why?
C: why?

Age: 3.5

M: which song did you do?
C: I gotten.
M: oh Sophie. You can't have forgotten already.
C: I have. Was so long. I gotten.

M: Daddy said he could hear you. At Matthew's. D'you know that?
C: it wasn't me.
M: wasn't it?

C: it was Matthew shouting.
M: was he being naughty?
C: mmm. And he was crying.

Task 2: Implications for Your Teaching

- In this chapter, we have looked at how a child develops English from the time of his birth to his pre-school age. From this, what implications can you draw for teaching English to children in Korea? Read the following list of example guidelines. Then make your own guidelines entitled "My Five Most Important Teaching Guidelines."

1. Let children develop English in their own way. Understand how children develop language.
2. Don't ask too much at first. Focus on listening, and let children develop their understanding skill.
3. Give children enough time to practice English speech sounds and use their speech organs. Provide correct and clear English for this.
4. Teach the words of the most familiar objects, persons, and actions first. Let the children communicate using these words from the beginning.
5. Focus on interaction. Speak as a communicator rather than as a teacher. Make yourself understood, and try to understand what children say.
6. Let children interact with each other in English as early as possible.
7. Avoid correcting mistakes and errors. Errors are an important part of children's language learning. Just give them correct and clear guidance and let them experiment with English freely. Acquiring grammar is the result of lots of experimenting with language.
8. Interacting is more important than error-correction. Give children a lot of encouragement and praise so that they interact in English.
9. Emphasize meaning and interaction rather than form and grammar. Without lots of speaking and listening, language learning does not take place.
10. Try to communicate with children in English from the beginning. Children need a lot of English input from the teacher.
11. Motivate children with pictures, games, stories and songs. Make lessons fun and interesting. Let them enjoy learning English.

12. Use visual materials like TVs, computers, and VTRs. Ask a lot of easy and simple questions using these.

<u>My Five Most Important Teaching Guidelines</u>

Summary

In this chapter, we have considered:

- ***The definition of L1 acquisition.*** Acquiring a language means that the speaker can control the five aspects of the language: phonology, vocabulary, grammar, discourse, and socio-linguistics. Phonology, vocabulary and grammar concern knowledge about language, and some specific skills, whereas discourse and socio-linguistics concern, more directly, the skills of using language for communication.
- ***Speech organs of infants.*** New-born babies remain unable to communicate in a spoken language for several months. They speak their first word when their speech organs fully develop and become physically fit for speech. This implies that children need a period of time to listen to the target language sounds and to exercise their speech organs.
- ***Three views on language development.*** There are three views about the language development of children, the nativist view, empiricist view and interactionist view. Nativists think that children develop a language because they have an innate ability to learn it. Empiricists think that the language development is the result of the circumstances in which children

are nurtured. Interactionists argue that the language development of children is the result of the interaction between the children and circumstances as well as their innate ability.

- ***The process of L1 acquisition and how children develop their native language.*** Children go through a set of stages when they learn a language: pre-linguistic (listening) stage, single word utterance stage, two-word utterance stage, and pre-school period.
- ***The teaching guidelines drawn from L1 acquisition.*** Children need to listen to and speak a language in order to develop it. The interaction between a mother and a young child shows that the focus is on meaning and keeping the conversation going. Errors and mistakes children produce in their utterances are ongoing in language development.

Useful Internet Sites

1. Teaching principles of second language acquisition
   - http://www.kapee.org/file/01-nkh.htm

2. Second language acquisition
   - http://www.dibsnara.com/ja-ryo-sil/lang-supduk.htm
   - http://my.dreamwiz.com/silan/child/uno.htm
   - http://www.mknest.org/mkj/10/ce_010.htm

References and Additional Resources

Benedict, H. (1979). Early lexical development: Comprehension and production. *Journal of Child Language, 48,* 1009-1018.

Boysson-Bardies, B. (1999). *How language comes to children.* Cambridge: The MIT Press.

Hoff-Ginsberg, E. (1997). *Language development.* New York: Brooks/Cole Publishing Company.

Ingram, D. (1989). *First language acquisition.* Cambridge: Cambridge University Press.

Peccei, J. S. (1994). *Child language.* London: Routledge.

Smith, M. (1926). An investigation of the development of the sentence and the extent of vocabulary in young children. *University of Iowa Studies in Child Welfare, 1*(5).

Tabors, P. O. (1997). *One child, two languages.* Baltimore: Paul H. Brooks.

Chapter 2
Second Language Acquisition

Chapter Two starts with a reflection on the ideal context for language learning, and presents information on how children acquire a second language. The main attention is given to detailing the stages of ESL development. The assumptions underlying the description of ESL development are that (1) children develop a second language by going through a set of stages, and (2) children develop a foreign language in a similar way when they are placed in a rich language learning environment. In this chapter, you will see how ESL development is similar to L1 development.

In this chapter, we will consider:
(1) What is the ideal context for learning English?
(2) What are the main stages of ESL development?
(3) How is ESL development similar to L1 development?

Task 1: Reflect

- What is the ideal context in which children learn English? Parents and teachers often think that the ideal situation for a child to learn English is to live in a country where the language is spoken. They believe that children living in an English-speaking country acquire English naturally through using it everyday.
- Compare these two situations. Which do you think is the more ideal? Why?

(1) Seyoung is a ten-year-old Korean girl. Her parents are living in the United States. She goes to an American public school. After one year she has picked up quite a lot of English from her classmates and from the playmates who live next door. She can chat happily with other children. She often translates for her mother when they go shopping together.

(2) Jinho is an eleven-year-old boy who lives in Seoul in Korea. He learns English at school. He does not hear or use any English outside school.

He is not sure why he is learning English. He simply knows his parents think learning English is important. He has been learning English for three years, but he knows few English words.

◆ The ideal context for learning English is ______________________
____
____

Children in EFL, ESL Schools

1. Children in EFL Schools

- Foreign language learning is different from second language learning. It is different in terms of the amount of exposure and the type of exposure to the language (Cameron, 2001. p.11). Children learning English as a foreign language (EFL) have limited opportunities to practice and experience English. Their encounter with English is a few hours of weekly teaching in the classroom, where English is not used as the language of instruction in any class other than English class. In addition, the children are not exposed to English in the street or at home. They do not face people using English for daily life purposes. Hence they have little chance to develop communicative skills in English.
- Furthermore, EFL programs for children have quite weak learning goals (McLaughlin, 1985). The programs tend to focus on acquiring basic listening and speaking skills and developing cultural awareness. Because of the limited teaching time and the setting, students hardly develop advanced oral skills, let alone communicative competence.

2. Children in ESL Schools

- ESL children are those who have already acquired their L1 and are in the process of learning English as a second language. They are different from EFL children in that they learn English in a natural setting where they are exposed to the daily use of English.
- In many ESL schools, students and teachers are native speakers of English and English is used as the language of interaction. In some settings, students come from a non-English background and the teacher provides English language input to the children. ESL schools, however, have one thing in common: the primary language used is English. Students have a good chance to develop English in a naturally communicative setting, and little chance to use their L1 in the classroom.
- Table 1 is adapted from Tabors (1997). EFL and ESL school settings are compared in this table.

Table 1. EFL and ESL Schools

Factors	EFL schools	ESL schools
Teachers	Native speakers of L1	Native speakers of English
Children	Native speakers of L1	Native speakers of English and/or native speakers of L1
Classroom interaction	In L1 and/or English	In English
Language outcome	Partial development of English and L1	Full development of English; no development of L1

- This table shows the contrast between EFL and ESL schools. In EFL schools both the teachers and students are native speakers of L1. The primary language for classroom interaction is L1, or both English and L1 are used. Since the EFL teacher does not provide the intensive language input that the ESL teacher does, children have little chance of developing English naturally.
- When we compare the two types of English-learning settings, we might think that children learn English better in an ESL setting than in an EFL

setting. In fact, many parents and educators think that their children will learn to speak English better if they go to an ESL school; if children are exposed sufficiently to the new language, and mingle with host language children socially. In the following section, you will look at how ESL children learn English in a natural setting.

Second Language Acquisition

1. Korean ESL Children

- We have met several Korean parents and their children who have lived in the US. Most of the parents told that their children had gone through painful experiences in order to learn to speak English. They said that for them and for their children, the advancement in English was like a battle. It cost them lots of time, energy, pain and patience. Some of the parents said that their children's ESL learning progress was surprisingly slow and tedious. Very often the parents were embarrassed, frustrated and even annoyed at the slow progress of their children.
- One of the parents who had a daughter in Grade 3 said,

  "My daughter came to the US three years ago. She was a happy child in Korea, but unhappy once she began school in the US. Looking back on it, the first six months at the school were a most difficult time for both of us. After six months, she slowly began to understand what was going on in the classroom, and did not suffer from her school life any more. She became a happy child again. I guess time cured my daughter's English problems."

- For the majority of Korean children living in the US, learning English is a long and difficult task. It is often accompanied by anger, self-blame, embarrassment, and frustration. Overcoming such affective obstacles is also a part of the process of ESL learning.

2. Tabors' Observation of ESL Children

- Tabors' two-year study of ESL nursery school children contains data which gives us a glimpse of the painful experiences of children's ESL learning. Tabors closely observed 15 children (ranging in age from 3 to 5 years) in nursery school classrooms for two years, and reported on their development in English. According to Tabors, ESL children undergo several stages of improvement in the new language. At first, the children often face isolation and are ignored by their classmates. Later they build up their L2 and become more involved in play activities.
- In Tabors' study, Byong-sun (a four-year old Korean boy) was observed spending his time, socially isolated from the rest of his classmates. During the free play period, he worked alone with Lego pieces, without asking for help. The other children in the classroom ignored him, and he rarely protested. He was treated by his playmates as a socially irrelevant member of the class.
- It is not astonishing that Byong-sun was playing alone, isolated from the other children. He knew very little English. When he tried to communicate verbally, he was not understood; nor did he understand his friends and teachers on many occasions. This linguistic constraint drove him naturally into social isolation, which gave him little chance of learning English through social interaction. Frequent social interaction of an ESL child with his peer group is crucial for his acquisition of a new language.
- Certainly there were also times when Byong-sun was able to communicate in English. When he named the things in the classroom, or counted the numbers of cards in a box, or drew a picture, he successfully communicated. These are low-pressure situations where ESL children are able to show off their proficiency in English using the simple words and skills they already possess. However, by and large, Byong-sun did not participate in peer group interactions during a substantial period of time.

♦ **Low-pressure situations**: the situations in which the child uses simple English to communicate. Art, music, math, PE classes are good examples.

- According to Tabors, the portrait of Byong-sun reveals the classic *double bind* that those who are learning a new language frequently face: in order to learn a new language, children must be socially accepted by those who speak the language; but to be socially accepted, they must already be able to speak the new language. In other words, in any language-learning situation of a natural type, communicative competence and social acceptance are strongly interrelated. These ESL children are in a double bind. The double bind is that each talent is necessary for the development of the other.

3. Garnica's Theory of the Omega Child

- Tabors' concept of the double bind is closely related to the concept of the omega child suggested by Garnica (1983). Garnica (1983) described children who are socially ineffective as omega children because they lack communicative and social competence. In Garnica's study which focused on six kindergarten children, the omega children were observed to engage in fewer child-child conversations and to have fewer conversational turns. They rarely participated in verbal interactions with other children. The exchanges that occurred were short.
- Furthermore, the omega children were infrequently addressed by other children. While non-omega children were addressed 9~16 times on the average, omega children were addressed 0~2 times on the average. However, the amount of private speech produced by omega children was much greater than that of non-omega children.
- This theory of omega children indicates that linguistic/communicative competence is closely related to social acceptance. If a child is not a good communicator, his peers make it hard for him to get into social situations. They ignore him. This tough and unpleasant experience can have a good effect. The child may become strongly motivated to learn L2 in order to escape from social isolation. This shows rather painfully what ESL children may go through in English-speaking classrooms.

♦ **Omega child**: Omega is the last letter of the Greek alphabet. Omega child refers to the child whose social position is extremely low in a group. The opposite is alpha child.

The Learning Stages of ESL Children

- When ESL children arrive in a classroom where English is used primarily, they are at the starting point of a new developmental pathway. The theories of the double bind and the omega child show what ESL children experience in the earlier stages of their ESL acquisition.
- Researchers note that ESL children primarily develop a new language in this sequence: home language use, silent period, use of telegraphic/formulaic expressions, and productive use of the new language.

1. Home Language Use

- Children continue to use their home language in the ESL setting. Read the following description of two ESL children in the US.

  (1) "Leandro, a Brazilian boy, during his first day in the English-speaking classroom, spoke in Portuguese. But no one else spoke Portuguese. At lunch time, he tried some yogurt and then pushed it away telling the teacher something in Portuguese. The teacher said he could not understand. After lunch Leandro asked Joanna something in Portuguese. She shook her head and said she did not understand. He did not seem distressed and continued to speak in Portuguese."

  (2) "Naoshi was from Japan. She tried to speak Japanese to Ling Ling (Chinese) and Byong-sun (Korean). Neither of them responded to her in Japanese. She tried to speak to Asian children in Japanese."

- Saville-Troike (1987) termed the use of home language in ESL settings "dilingual discourse." By using dilingual discourse, children continued to speak their home language as if those around them could understand them. The younger children used dilingual discourse over lengthier periods of time than the older children. Dilingual discourse is often effective when the child speaks to another in a simple, low-pressure situation.

♦ **Dilingual discourse** refers to the discourse or utterances that the speaker can understand, but the hearer cannot.

2. Silent, Non-Verbal Period

- When children discover their home language does not work any more, they stop talking altogether, and keep silent. During this silent period, they collect information about the new language and spend time experimenting with sounds. Tabors (1997) calls this the non-verbal period. Children in this period play with other children, but they prefer to communicate non-verbally. The following cases describe children during their silent period.

  (1) **Six-month silence:** Hakuta (1978) observed a Japanese girl who arrived in the United States in October, but did not speak English until the next April. She played with English-speaking friends, but she did not produce any English for about six months.
  (2) **1½ -year silence:** Tabors (1982) reported on a Greek boy (5 years old) who began to speak English after a year and a half in a child care center.
  (3) **One-semester silence:** Leo (Kim, 2003), a seven-year old Korean boy, kept silent during his first semester in a US school. He did not talk to his English-speaking classmates in English at all. He did not try to speak English to his family at all. Both at home and school he did not attempt to speak English. From the second semester, however, after summer vacation, he began to speak some English phrases in the classroom.

- This silent period seems to be a consistent feature of the ESL children's learning process. Children suddenly stop talking, and attempt to communicate by non-verbal means like gestures, facial expressions and drawings. While keeping silent, the children focus on getting familiar with speech sounds and learning basic vocabulary for communication.

◆ **Silent period:** The 'silent period hypothesis' implies that children need some time to develop the skill of understanding basic English. Children tend to keep silent in order to focus on listening and to develop their listening skill.

3. Use of Telegraphic/Formulaic Speech

- Children soon begin to produce simple words and phrases. At first they use telegraphic and formulaic speech. Telegraphic speech is speech in which children use a few content words as an utterance. At this stage, they depend primarily on the names of objects to interact with English speakers. These examples show telegraphic speech (T: teacher, S: student).

(1) T: What's this?
S: Bridge.
T: Yes, it's a bridge.

(2) T: Count from one to ten.
S: One, two,…

- Formulaic speech is speech in which children use chunks of words or phrases they already know. It is different from ordinary speech in that the speaker uses it, without understanding its structure.
- Borah, a 3rd grade child, used the pattern, 'where + noun', in her conversation with her homeroom teacher. It was found that she used the structure, without knowing the exact meaning of the word 'where'.

(3) S: Where homework? (What is homework?)
T: Not today. You have no homework.

(4) S: Where two thousand spelling? (How do you write 'two thousand'?
T: What?
S: Where two thousand. I don't know.
T: You don't know how to write 'two thousand'?

- As Examples (1) ~(4) show, at the initial stage of production, ESL children do not exactly understand the meaning of some of the English words and grammar. Hence, they combine the words and phrases which they already know with words which they think are related to the meaning they intend to express. We call this telegraphic, formulaic speech.
- By using such speech, children experiment with words and phrases. This becomes the foundation of their grammar development.

4. Productive Use of ESL

- Soon children begin to use the language productively. When they have acquired enough words and phrases, children no longer repeat formulaic phrases or names of people and things. They begin to speak creatively, producing their own sentences. As in the following 'frames and slots' sentences, children generate a variety of creatively constructed expressions.

(5) I want <u>my mommy.</u>
a play dough.
an ice cream

- By using English ingeniously, they analyze the language and begin to make guesses about how the language is built. It is not surprising that they make many mistakes as they experiment with sentence construction and improve their grammar base.

Task 2: Implications for Your Teaching

1. If you were a parent of Byong-sun, described in this chapter, what home assistance would you give him?

2. Compare ESL developmental stages with L1 developmental stages, and match them. What implications for EFL teaching do you draw from this comparison?

    (1) Home language use
    (2) Silent period
    (3) Telegraphic/Formulaic phrase use
    (4) Productive use of ESL

(a) Pre-linguistic period
(b) One-word utterance
(c) Two-word utterance
(d) Pre-school period

3. Look at Table 1 in this chapter again, and think about the learning stages of ESL development. Describe five or more implications for your classroom teaching.

(1) Teach English in English. Give rich language input.

(2) Accept the mistakes children produce as a part of their natural language development.

(3) ______________________________

(4) ______________________________

(5) ______________________________

(6) ______________________________

(7) ______________________________

Summary

In this chapter, we have considered:

- **The ideal context for children's English learning.** Many people think that children can learn English more easily and more successfully when they go to school in an English-speaking country (ESL school). ESL schools are different from EFL schools in terms of teacher, students, classroom interaction and learning outcome. As an EFL teacher, it is your job to strengthen ESL elements and reduce EFL elements in your English classroom.
- **The omega child.** Children do not learn a new language without difficulty. ESL children, when they are first placed in an EFL context, suffer from isolation from the main stream group and have a lot of communication problems. Omega children refer to those ESL children who are socially isolated in the classroom. Language learning takes place while they try hard to overcome these problems.
- **The learning stages of ESL children.** Like L1 children, ESL children develop English by going through a set of stages; for example, home language use, a silent period, use of formulaic/telegraphic expressions, and creative use of ESL. This suggests that EFL children need to have a chance to go through a similar set of stages in order to develop their English successfully.

Useful Internet Sites

1. Second language development in children
   - http://www.1-language.com/eslarticles/foster-l2-children.htm

2. Writing development of ESL children
   - http://www.midtesol.org/Newsletter/20040210LeeArticle.htm

References and Additional Resources

Cameron, L. (2001). *Teaching languages to young learners.* Cambridge: Cambridge University Press.

Garnica, O. (1983). Social dominance and conversational interaction: The omega child in the classroom. In C. Wallat & J. Green (Eds.), *Ethnography and language in educational settings.* Norwood, NJ: Ablex Publishing.

Hakuta, K. (1978). A report on the development of grammatical morphemes in a Japanese girl learning English as a second language. In E. Hatch (Ed.), *Second language acquisition: A book of readings.* Rowley, MA: Newbury House Publishers.

Kim, J. (2003). Language development of a Korean ESL child. *Primary English Education, 9*(1), 200-224.

McLaughlin, B. (1985). *Second language acquisition in childhood.* Hillsdale, NJ: Lawrence Erlbaum Associates.

Moon, J. (2000). *Children learning English.* Oxford: Macmillian Heinemann English Language Teaching.

Saville-Troike, M. (1987). Dilingual discourse: The negotiation of meaning without a common code. *Linguistics, 25,* 81-106.

Tabors, P. O. (1997). *One child, two languages.* Baltimore: Paul. H. Brookes.

Chapter 3
Teaching Methods

Chapter Three presents the characteristics of the major teaching methods. It starts by showing how teachers' views about learning English affect the way they teach in the classroom. Attention is given to reviewing traditional as well as recent teaching methods and providing principles of English teaching. You will apply your understanding, of teaching methods in general, to teaching English to children.

In this chapter, we will consider:

(1) What are the major teaching methods?
(2) How is language viewed in each of the teaching methods?
(3) What are the components of communicative competence?
(4) What are the principles of English teaching suggested by Brown?

Task 1: Reflect

- Teachers' views about learning English affect the way they teach. For example, many teachers feel that it is very difficult to teach English to children at the primary level. To make things easier, they use translation as their main teaching method. They can't imagine how children could learn English without translation. Thus, translation, they believe, is necessary to the success of English teaching in the primary classroom.
- Compare the outlines of the two lessons below. How does each of the teachers think children should learn English? What beliefs does each teacher have? Describe your opinion, using the following list.

1. What is a language?
   (1) Teacher A: ______________________________
   (2) Teacher B: ______________________________
   (3) You: ______________________________

2. What does learning a language mean?
   (1) Teacher A: ______________________________
   (2) Teacher B: ______________________________
   (3) You: ______________________________

3. What is the best method to teach English?
   (1) Teacher A: ______________________________
   (2) Teacher B: ______________________________
   (3) You: ______________________________

- Teacher A

1) Presentation: The teacher presents each preposition through showing an example.

   The ruler is in the box.
   The ruler is under the box.
   The ruler is on the table.
   The ruler is near the table.

2) Whole-class repetition: Students repeat the sentences after the teacher.
3) Group drill: The teacher points to objects and gets groups of students to describe their location.

   T: Group A, where is the pencil?
   G_A: It's in the box.
   T: Group B, where is the ruler?
   G_B: It's under the table.

- Teacher B

1) Warm-up game/review: The teacher calls four pupils to the front of the class. He lets them carry out some instructions in pairs. The rest of the class guesses which pair will be fastest in following the instructions.

   Put the ruler in the box.
   Put the pencil on the table.
   Put the eraser under the box.

2) Dialog: The teacher places objects in different locations. With the help

of the pupils, he elicits questions and answers.

Where is the ruler?

It's in the box.

3) Communication game: Pupils work in pairs and fill in the missing objects on a picture. There are two versions of the picture so that Pupil A has the objects that Pupil B does not have.

Pupil A	Pupil B
A. Ask your partner a question and draw the missing things. Missing things: pencil, ruler, eraser	B. Ask your partner a question and draw the missing things. Missing things: dog, cap, book

Traditional Teaching Methods

1. The Grammar-Translation Method

- For many centuries, languages were taught using the Grammar-Translation Method in which the teacher's medium of instruction was the native language, with little active use of the target language.
- Around the Renaissance period, Latin and Greek were taught because it was thought that

the study of grammar was good for mental training. Reading and translating texts, together with the study of grammar, were the essence of language learning.

- The main characteristics of this method are as follows:

(1) Written language is emphasized over spoken language.
(2) Reading and writing are the basic skills. In contrast, little or no attention is paid to listening and speaking. Pronunciation also receives little attention.
(3) Vocabulary and grammar are emphasized. Much vocabulary is taught in the form of lists of isolated words. Grammar is taught deductively. Little attention is paid to the content of texts, which are treated as exercises in grammatical analysis.
(4) The activities are mainly based on teacher-student interaction. Students will have little or no opportunity to use the target language.
(5) The teacher puts great emphasis on developing accuracy. The students have high anxiety when producing spoken language, since the teacher immediately corrects their errors, if any.
(6) Translation is a common technique for the teacher to use in the classroom. Students spend their time translating written texts line by line. The teacher uses translation in the evaluation of students.

> ♦ **Grammar-translation method**: Emphasis on learning reading and writing; little attention to pronunciation and oral skills; memorization of vocabulary items; deductive learning of grammar; lots of teacher-student interaction; emphasis on developing accuracy; line-by-line translation.

2. The Direct Method

- The Direct Method is based on Francois Gouin's idea that foreign language learning should be like first language learning. Gouin was a teacher of Latin and, based on his observations of child language learning, published *The Art of Learning and Studying Foreign Language* in 1880. His method is called the Series Method. He is the forerunner of the Direct Method.
- Emphasis on oral speech and the rejection of translation are the hallmarks of the direct method. The name "Direct Method" was coined at the end of 19th century (McLaughlin, 1985).

- Charles Berlitz, a strong advocate of the Direct Method, argued that the learner must use the target language constantly without using the first language.
- The main characteristics of this method are as follows:

(1) Learners learn a foreign language directly, i.e. without translation. In other words, the teacher doesn't use students' native language.
(2) The teacher is a fluent speaker of the target language, and the teacher's correct pronunciation is emphasized.
(3) First, spoken language (speaking and listening) is taught and, then, written language (reading and writing).
(4) Common everyday speech is emphasized and dialogues are frequently used in lessons.
(5) Classroom activities include student-student interaction, along with teacher-student and student-teacher interaction.
(6) Grammatical rules are not taught directly. The teacher teaches grammar inductively, i.e. by examples and visual demonstration.
(7) Classes are small (not more than 10).

> ◆ **Direct method**: Rejection of translation; emphasis on the teacher's correct pronunciation; emphasis on spoken language; learning of everyday speech; inductive grammar instruction; small class size.

3. The Audio-Lingual Method

- This method was popular in the 1950s and 1960s. It is based on behaviorist psychology which relies on conditioning and habit-formation models of learning.
- The principles behind the behaviorist learning theory are simple. Look at the diagram of a rat in a maze (adapted from Hubbard, et.al, 1983).

- If the food is placed in the right-hand side of the maze consistently, the rat will find the food quickly after several trials. We can say here that a habit is formed;

  i.e., a habit is formed when a correct response to a stimulus is consistently rewarded.

- Habit formation is the result of stimulus, correct response, and reward occurring together again and again. According to Skinner, reward is much more effective than punishment in a teaching situation. He says that a teacher should arrange a task so that the learners have a good chance of getting the answer right. In his view, a teaching program should be split up into a series of very simple steps. Once the student has succeeded in getting one step right, he can go on to the next.
- Here is an example of behaviorist learning theory applied to English teaching (Hubbard et al, 1983).

  T: (Holds up a book) Book. Book. Repeat! (stimulus: object and sound)
  S: Book. (correct response)
  T: Good! (reward)

  T: (Holds up a book) What's this? (stimulus: object and sound)
  S: Book. (correct response)
  T: Good! (reward)

♦ Can you think of an approach, other than "Good!" that the teacher might use as positive reinforcement?

- The main characteristics of this method are as follows:

  (1) A language is considered a set of habits and language learning is basically habit-formation. Students' successful responses are positively reinforced. Their errors are avoided to prevent bad habit-formation.
  (2) Language skills are learned more effectively if oral skills precede written skills. Hence the students need to develop the four skills in this order: listening, speaking, reading and writing.
  (3) Language is speech, not writing (frequent use of tapes, labs, visual aids

are needed). Spoken language is learned prior to written language.

(4) Language materials are presented in dialogue form, since dialogues (everyday speech) are very useful for developing aural-oral skills.

(5) Language is acquired through drills (repetition, substitution, and transformation), memorization, and pattern practice. For example, structural patterns presented in dialogues are learned through imitation/mimicry and memorization without regard to meaning or context.

(6) Students learn grammar inductively.

(7) Phonological accuracy is emphasized through repetitive drills in the language laboratory. Correct pronunciation is taught from the beginning, using tapes, or visual aids.

(8) New vocabulary and structures are presented in the meaningful context of everyday situations.

(9) Both the teacher and the students are not permitted to use the native language.

(10) Languages are different. Understanding differences between the first language and the foreign language is helpful in learning the latter.

◆ **Audio-lingual method**: Stress on habit-formation; priority of spoken language over written language; emphasis on dialogues, drills, memorization, and pattern practice; inductive grammar learning; phonological accuracy through repetitive drills in the language laboratory; presentation of new vocabulary and structures in meaningful contexts; avoidance of students' native language; understanding differences between the first language and the foreign language.

- The major teaching techniques of the Audio-Lingual Method are as follows:

(1) Repetition

T: This is a pen.

S: This is a pen

(2) Inflection

T: I called the boy. (singular -> plural)

S: I called the boys.

T: I called the girl.

S: I called the girls.

(3) Replacement

T: I have a book.
a pen
S: I have a pen.
T: she
S: She has a pen.
T: a baby
S: She has a baby.

(4) Restatement

T: Ask Misuk how old she is.
S: How old are you?
T: Ask your partner how old he is.
S: How old are you?

(5) Completion

T: I'll eat my pizza and you eat yours.
S: I'll eat my pizza and you eat ________.
T: I'll go to my house and you go to ___________.
S: I'll go to my house and you go to ________.

(6) Transposition

T: I'm hungry.
So
S: So am I.
T: I'm tall.
So
S: So am I.

(7) Expansion

T: I know him. well
S: I know him well.
T: I know him well. very.
S: I know him very well.

(8) Contraction

T: Come to the library.

S: Come here.

(9) Transformation

T: I have a book. not

S: I don't have a book.

T: They have books. not.

S: They don't have books.

(10) Integration

T: I have a pencil. It's red.

S: I have a red pencil.

T: I have a bag. It's blue.

S: I have a blue bag.

4. Communicative Language Teaching

1) A New Teaching Theory

- **Language as a system of rules**: Until the 1950s and 1960s language was seen as a system of syntactic rules and the task of language learners was to acquire these rules. During this period, linguists were concerned with describing language in terms of rules and patterns. The aim of language learning was to master the structures of the language, so language specialists emphasized that instructions should focus on teaching basic sentence patterns.
- **Language as a system of meaning**: However, during the 1970s, language began to be seen as a system for the expression of meaning and linguists started to analyze language as a system for the expression of meaning, rather than as a system of syntactic rules. This view of language as a system of expressing meaning has had a strong effect on language teaching. If language is a system for expressing meaning, the focus must be on learners expressing meaning effectively. Thus communicative activities and games have become very common in the language classroom. In particular, this view of language learning has had a profound effect on syllabus design and textbook writing. This era was the beginning of communicative language teaching (CLT).

2) Components of Communicative Competence

- What does an L1 speaker know about his native language? During 1970s linguists and educators began to redefine and reevaluate language itself. Hymes (1972) states that the L1 speaker's ability to communicate competently entails knowing not only the rules of grammar, but also the rules of use. For example, compare these two utterances.

  (1) Open the window.
  (2) Would you open the window, please?

- We use Example (1) when we ask a close friend, and use Example (2) when we ask a stranger or a less intimate adult. Producing these sentences correctly concerns the rules of grammar (grammatical competence). How we use these utterances appropriately concerns the rules of use (sociolinguistic competence).
- Canale and Swain (1980) expanded Hymes' view on language. They define communicative competence as involving four different components: grammatical competence, sociolinguistic competence, discourse competence and strategic competence.

- **Grammatical competence**: Grammatical competence enables speakers to understand and accurately produce words and grammatical structures. It allows speakers to connect words into utterances, using accurate structures. Due to grammatical competence, speakers are able to understand and effectively produce a great number of utterances.
- **Sociolinguistic competence**: Sociolinguistic competence enables speakers to perform such speech acts as: *greetings, thanks, and apologies.* They know the etiquette and routines associated with these speech acts. For example, "How much money do you make?" is an impolite question in European countries; but it can be a polite expression in some Asian countries. The social meaning of an expression can be different from culture to culture. Sociolinguistic competence includes the speaker's cultural understanding of the target language.
- **Discourse competence**: Discourse competence enables speakers to open and close a conversation, to take a turn during a conversation, and to use discourse markers. Discourse competence includes the ability to successfully connect utterances and make them clear beyond the sentence level. Some discourse markers are:

(1) To show time relationships: after/before this, then, at that time, until…
(2) To indicate cause: so, because
(3) To show contrast: but, however
(4) To change topic: by the way

- **Strategic competence**: Strategic competence allows speakers to communicate in their own language. If they don't know a word (e.g. elephant), they use gestures or combine two or more related words (big nosed animal), and keep the conversation going.
- According to Canale and Swain's definition of communicative competence, practicing grammar at sentence level is not enough to give a learner communicative competence. He/She needs additional practice to acquire sociolinguistic, discourse, and strategic competence (i.e., the skill to use the language) as well as grammatical competence (i.e., knowledge about the language).

◆ **Grammatical competence**: the ability to make sentences by connecting words; **discourse competence**: the ability to make texts by connecting sentences; **sociolinguistic competence**: the ability to speak appropriately according to the hearer; **strategic competence**: the ability to keep a conversation going.

3) Characteristics of CLT

- CLT is based on the definition of the term 'communicative competence.' The characteristics of CLT are as follows:

(1) The goal of CLT is to have students become communicatively competent in the use of the language. So classroom goals are not only focused on grammatical and discourse competence, but also on socio-linguistic and strategic competence. CLT also emphasizes four language skills from the beginning.
(2) Both fluency and accuracy are aims to be developed according to the CLT approach. If the aim of a certain activity is to develop fluency, the teacher must prompt communication between and among the students, acting as a manager of the activity, a facilitator of learning,

or a co-communicator. Students may make lots of errors in communicating with each other. In CLT, the errors of students are seen as a natural outcome of their development of communicative skills.

(3) The students in CLT are encouraged to use the target language. So they participate in many communicative activities such as role-plays, games, and tasks.

(4) Students need to have knowledge of form and meaning and function when learning the target language. Language function (e.g., how to greet) is emphasized over form (e.g., grammar). Therefore, a functional syllabus is more preferable to a grammatical syllabus.

(5) Authentic materials (e.g., movies, dramas) are used in class, since the teacher should help develop students' fluency and their socio-linguistic competence. These materials include lots of cultural information. Culture is the representation of the everyday lifestyle of native speakers.

(6) The students' native language has no particular role in CLT. Students are led to realize that the target language is a vehicle for communication.

(7) Evaluation is quite differently achieved in the communicative classroom. The teacher evaluates not only students' accuracy, but also their fluency. To evaluate fluency, the teacher can informally evaluate the students' performance, and then formally use an integrative test which has a communicative function.

5. Total Physical Response (TPR)

- James Asher (1965) proposed what is called "the TPR method"; an innovative method of language instruction. According to Asher, about 50% of all speech directed at a 12-month-old infant involves commands; and responding to these commands physically is an important feature of the child's early language acquisition. TPR, based on such commands and responses to them, has these two guidelines:

(1) Teach students with a format in which they listen and respond physically to commands.
(2) Encourage students to listen and observe first. Don't ask them to speak right from the beginning.

- Guidelines (1) and (2) mean that students are not required to say anything at the beginning. They are advised to respond physically to spoken language in the form of commands. It is assumed that children develop their comprehensive skills (listening, reading) before they develop their productive skills (speaking, writing). To carry on Guidelines (1) and (2), thus, the teacher becomes an active person, directing the behavior of all the students.
- This teaching method is based upon the way children learn their first language. In a TPR classroom, the teacher delays the teaching of speaking until the students establish their comprehension skills. This is called "delayed oral production." Students' oral production is delayed in order for them to feel free of tension. However, it should be noted that the students' native language would be rarely used in this method.
- Here are some examples of using this technique with young children:

(1) Present action words (Stand up. Sit down. Walk. Turn. Run. Jump.).
(2) Learners perform the actions in response to simple commands.

Stand up.
Sit down.
Walk.
Turn.
Run.
Jump.

(3) Increase the information in these commands. For example,

Stand up, pick up the pencils and put them on the chair.
Walk to the door, pick up the pencil, and sit down on the chair.
Mira, stand up, pick up a picture of a tall man and put it next to a picture of a cow.

6. The Natural Approach

- Krashen and Terrell (1983) suggested the Natural Approach. This approach is based on the research of input and its relationship to child language acquisition. The research on language input for children indicates: children receive input from their parents which is well-tuned to their linguistic needs. Parents simplify or clarify their speech and help their children learn their native language more easily (See Chapter 1).

- The main goal of the natural approach is to develop students' ability for basic communication. Krashen and Terrell assume that all students go through the same stages of language acquisition. The first stage is a silent stage in which students are simply exposed to English. During this silent stage, learners should not be forced to speak. Like the TPR method, the Natural Approach focuses on listening during the initial stage of language learning.
- In the Natural Approach, the initial task of the teacher is to provide comprehensible input. Comprehensible input is defined as input that is slightly beyond the learner's current level of proficiency.

◆ **Comprehensible input**: A level of language which is not far beyond the level of the learner; thus language which the learner can process.

- When speech emerges, students use one or two-word utterances to respond to questions and communicate their ideas. Errors are not corrected so that learners remain free from stress. It is assumed that learners gradually correct their errors as they receive more input and develop their speaking proficiency.
- The principles of the natural approach are as follows (Terrell, 1981):

  (1) The learner must receive "comprehensible input." That is, the child must be able to understand the essential meaning of the communication.
  (2) Speech must contain a message and there must be a need to communicate that message. Sentences that are taught to children in

order to demonstrate a rule of grammar will not help the child use the rule in speech. Reading and writing are taught as natural extensions of listening and speaking.

(3) No attempt should be made to force production before children are ready. A period of three to six months is necessary for children learning a new language to develop their understanding.

(4) The language-learning environment should be free of tension. Children will learn only if they feel secure affectively. They should feel free to experiment creatively with the new language.

7. Learner-Centered Approach

- One of the most nagging questions in language teaching is "Why don't learners learn what teachers teach?" Whatever teaching method teachers use, there tends to be a gap between the things teachers try to get their students to learn and the things that the students actually learn. Learner-centered education is designed to narrow down this gap by seeing things from the learner's point of view.
- In a learner-centered classroom, the decisions about what will be taught, how it will be taught, when it will be taught, and how it will be assessed will be made with reference to the learner (Nunan, 1999, p.11). Learners are encouraged to make decisions by themselves. By making such decisions, learners will have some control over their learning. However, since very few students have the ability to make choices about their learning, they can only do this with the assistance and guidance of the teacher. The duty of the teacher is to encourage and assist his/her learners to move toward the fully autonomous end of the pedagogical continuum as:

  Teacher-centered ←——————→ Learner-centered

- **Intake**: Corder (1967) suggested the notion of *intake*. According to Corder, *intake* is what the learner processes. Intake facilitates language development. When the input is given (*input* is what is given to the learner), only a small portion of this input becomes as intake. Figure 1 shows this.

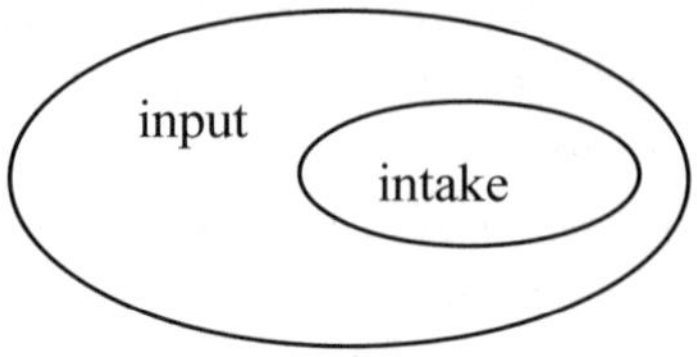

Figure1. The input and intake

- It is known that L1 children unconsciously internalize and then experiment with the patterns they hear in speech. This means that they receive input and absorb some of it as intake. In the same way, ESL/EFL students may internalize English vocabulary and grammar when they are exposed to written and spoken English. However, not all input leads to language development. Students process a part of the input and internalize it. It is like our digestive system: input is like eating food, and intake is like digesting food. The question is how we can provide input so that learners process as much of it as possible.
- Learner-centered education aims to increase the intake of the learner by encouraging students to decide what they learn, and how they learn. They are guided to be responsible for what they learn. The assumption here is that students process input more effectively and have more intake if they are exposed to what they really need and want.

8. Task-Based Approach

- In this approach, students are presented with a task they have to solve, instead of a language structure. Hence, the focus of the lesson is on the task, not on the structure.
- Recently, a task-based approach to language teaching has become popular among ESL/EFL educators. Nunan (1999) draws a distinction between real-world tasks and pedagogical tasks.

1) Real-world tasks

- Tasks are pieces of work undertaken for oneself or for others. They include the hundreds of things people do in everyday life; painting a fence, dressing a child, and buying a bag are examples. These tasks are the things that we do outside the classroom in our daily life.
- The final goal of language teaching is to enable learners to do these things

using the target language. Thus, the principle underlying task-based learning is that learners learn language better by rehearsing the tasks that are directly related to performance outside the classroom. For example, learners rehearse the language and speech acts needed to open an account in a bank.

2) Pedagogical tasks

- Learners need to do many things in class that are not directly related to the daily tasks outside the classroom, e.g., listening to a tape, solving a crossword puzzle, and working in a group to solve a problem. It is assumed that these activities facilitate the development of a learner's language proficiency.
- A pedagogical task is a piece of classroom work that involves learners in practicing, understanding and speaking in the target language. Learners are led to express and convey meaning while carrying out the pedagogical tasks. Examples of these tasks are listening to instructions and drawing a picture, responding to a birthday party invitation, and describing one's family. By focusing on pedagogical tasks, learners are believed to develop certain aspects or skills related to the target language.

Principles of Language Teaching

- Some teachers complain that the development of teaching methods has not contributed to ESL/EFL teaching. No single method seems best.
- Recently, the concept of "the best method" is no longer a central issue in second language teaching. Instead, many ESL/EFL experts recommend that teachers need to take a principled approach to language teaching. For example, Brown (1994) suggested the following 10 principles which teachers should consider when they plan classroom tasks and activities:

(1) Lower inhibitions.
(2) Encourage risk taking.
(3) Build students' self-confidence.
(4) Help students develop intrinsic motivation.
(5) Promote cooperative learning.
(6) Encourage students to use right-brain processing.
(7) Promote ambiguity tolerance.

(8) Help students use their intuition.
(9) Get students to make their mistakes work for them.
(10) Get students to set their own goals.

Task 2: Practice

1. So far we have looked at various teaching methods. What do you think is the best teaching method for teaching English to children? Why?

2. Look at the activities below. Examine how recent teaching theories and methods are reflected in them.

(1) **Activity**

● 내가 살고 싶은 집 소개하기 활동을 해 봅시다.

This is my house.
This is a living room.
This is a kitchen.
This is a bedroom.

(2) A: What time is it in London?
B: It's three.

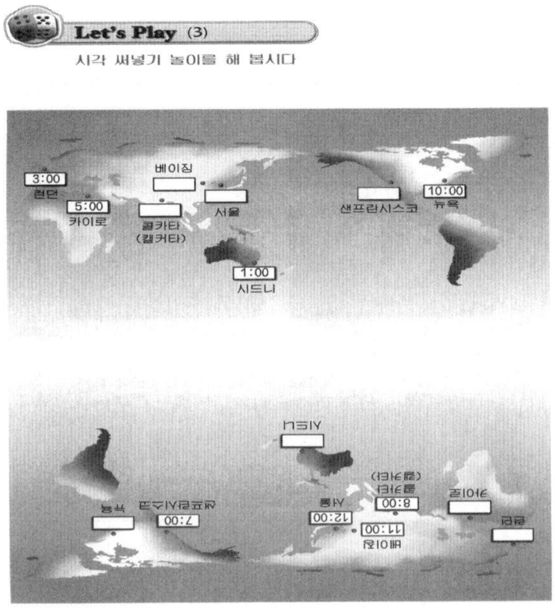

(3) Ask and answer with your partner.
A: What's c?
B: It's a big box.

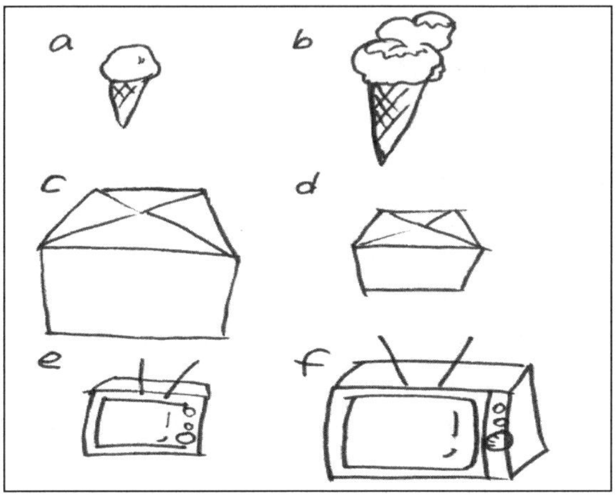

(4) Draw a picture of your family and tell your partner.

This is my father. He is a teacher.
This is my mother. She is a nurse.

Summary

In this chapter, we have considered:

- ***The traditional teaching methods.*** Among the traditional teaching methods are the grammar-translation method, the direct method, and the audio-lingual method.
- The main characteristics of ***the Grammar-Translation Method*** are: (1) Written language is emphasized over spoken language; (2) Much vocabulary is taught in the form of lists of isolated words; (2) Grammar is taught deductively; (4) Little attention is paid to the content of texts; (5) Accuracy is emphasized; (6) Students spend their time translating written texts line by line.
- The main characteristics of ***the Direct Method*** are: (1) The foreign language is taught directly without translation; (2) Spoken language is

taught first; (3) Grammar is taught inductively through examples and visual demonstration; (4) Classes are small (not more than 10).

- The main characteristics of ***the Audio-Lingual Method*** are: (1) Language learning is considered basically habit-formation; (2) Oral skills are emphasized; (3) Language materials are presented in dialogue form; (4) Language is taught through drills and pattern practice; (5) Students learn grammar inductively; (6) The teacher and the students rarely use the native language of the students.
- ***Components of Communicative Competence.*** During the 1970s, language began to be seen as a system for the expression of meaning. This view of language as a system of expressing meanings had a strong effect on language teaching. Canale and Swain (1980) defined communicative competence as involving four different components: grammatical competence, discourse competence, sociolinguistic competence, and strategic competence.
- ***Other Teaching Methods.*** Other teaching methods are Total Physical Response (TPR), Communicative Language Teaching (CLT), the Natural Approach, a learner-centered approach, and a task-based approach.
- ***Principles of Language Teaching.*** Brown (1994) suggested some principles on the basis of recent teaching theories and methods: (1) Lower inhibitions; (2) Encourage risk taking; (3) Build students' self-confidence; (4) Help students develop intrinsic motivation; (5) Promote cooperative learning; (6) Encourage students to use right-brain processing; (7) Promote ambiguity tolerance; (8) Help students use their intuition; (9) Get students to make their mistakes work for them; (10) Get students to set their own goals.

Useful Internet Sites

1. CAL resource guides online
   - http://www.cal.org/resources/digest/rodgers.html
2. TEFL methodology index
   - http://www.btinternet.com/~ted.power/teflindex.htm
3. English raven
   - http://www.englishraven.com/methodology.html

References and Additional Resources

Asher, J. (1965). The strategy of the total physical response: An application to learning Russian. *International Review of Applied Linguistics, 3*(4), 291-300.

Brown, D. (1994). *Principles of language learning and teaching.* Englewood Cliffs, NJ: Prentice Hall Regents.

Canale, M., & Swain, M. (1980). Theoretical bases of communicative approaches to second language teaching and testing. *Applied Linguistics, 1*(1), 1-47.

Corder, S. P. (1967). The significance of learner errors. *IRAL, 5,* 161-169.

Hubbard, P., Jones, H., Thornton, B., and Wheeler, R. (1983). *A training course for TEFL.* Oxford: Oxford University Press.

Hymes, (1972). Models of the interaction of language and social life. In U. Gumperz & D. Hymes (Eds.), *Directions in sociolinguistics: The ethnography of communication.* New York: Holt, Rinehart & Winston.

Krashen, S. D. (1981). The theoretical and practical relevance of simple codes in second language acquisition. In R. Scarcella & S. D. Krashen (Eds.), *Research in second language acquisition.* Rowley, MA: Newbury House.

Krashen, D., & Terrel, T. D. (1983). *The natural approach: Language acquisition in the classroom.* Oxford: Pergamon.

McLaughlin, B. (1985). *Second language acquisition in childhood.* Hillsdale, NJ: Lawrence Erlbaum Associates.

Nunan, D. (1999). *Second language teaching.* Boston, MA: Heinle & Heinle Publishers.

Terrel, T. D. (1981). The natural approach in bilingual education. In *Schooling and language minority students: A theoretical framework.* Los Angeles: California State University, Evaluation, Dissemination and Assessment Center.

Chapter 4
Learning Styles and Language Acquisition Hypotheses

Chapter Four presents the major learning styles and language acquisition hypotheses. In this chapter, you will understand how learners are different from one another in handling tasks (learning styles) and why you need to do a variety of learning activities in the classroom. In addition, the main hypotheses (or theories) are also presented in order to suggest that teachers need to have an active and flexible attitude when teaching a new language. The tasks included in this chapter offer you the chance to apply theory to classroom teaching.

In this chapter, we will consider:
(1) What are the major learning styles?
(2) What are the major language acquisition hypotheses?

Learning Styles

- The term "learning styles" means consistent and enduring tendencies or preferences which an individual has in learning something new.
- In general, students all have their own learning style. Some like to learn, and learn best through songs. Others like to roleplay. Still others like to read. Students use their own learning style when they learn a new language.
- Language learning styles are divided into the four dimensions: analytic-global styles, intuitive-sensory styles, sensory preferences (visual,

auditory, hands-on), and closure-open styles (Scarcella & Oxford, 1992).

1. Analytic ↔ Global

- Analytic learners like to distinguish parts from a whole, so they see only parts and not their relationship to the whole. You may often complain that analytic learners can't see the forest for the trees. In learning a language, they like concentrating on grammatical details, studying alone, reading newspapers, and doing exercises and drills. They are good at analyzing activities. However, they are not good at communicative activities.
- Global learners prefer to perceive the whole picture of a problem, an idea or an event. They tend to be sociable, so they like to do interactive, communicative activities. In language learning, they like to guess the meaning of a new word, to paraphrase, or to play games with their classmates.

2. Intuitive ↔ Sensory

- Intuitive learners are able to think in abstract ways. Most often they are fast learners and able to get the main principles of how the new language works.
- On the other hand, sensory learners are concerned with concrete facts. They are not good at thinking in abstract ways. Often they are slow learners, and abstract principles and rules are not important to them.

3. Sensory Preference (Visual ↔ Auditory ↔ Hands-on)

- Learners are different in their sensory preference. They are divided into visual, auditory, and hands-on learners. Visual learners are most comfortable with physical, perceptual learning activities. They like to read and get a great deal of visual stimulation from their reading. However, conversations, and oral directions without visual backup can be confusing to them.
- Auditory learners are comfortable with lectures, conversations and many other oral activities. They enjoy role-plays, songs and similar activities. Compared to visual learners, they more often have difficulty with written activities.
- Hands-on learners like lots of movement. They enjoy working with

objects, cards, and collages. Sitting at a desk for a long time is not for them. They like to have breaks and move around.

4. Closure ↔ Open

- Closure-oriented learners take language learning seriously. They prefer grammar rules and lesson directions and like to control their learning. Hence they want to have vocabulary lists and grammar rules before they play a game. They are not good at open-ended communication. They generally like task-based learning activities.
- Open-oriented learners take language learning far less seriously. They like to treat language learning like a game to be enjoyed. They are not worried about class deadlines. They are more concerned with having a good time in the language classroom.

A closure style

An open style

Task 1: Reflect

1. Talk about your learning styles using this scale.

Analytic ↔ Global
Intuitive ↔ Sensory
Visual ↔ Hands-on ↔ Auditory
Closure ↔ Open

2. Think about learning activities fit for each of the learning styles in the elementary English classroom.

    - Analytic:
    - Global:
    - Intuitive:
    - Visual:
    - Auditory:
    - Hands-on:
    - Closure:
    - Open:

Language Acquisition Hypotheses

- In this section, we will examine four different hypotheses concerning the relationship between classroom interaction and L2 learning: (1) the Simplified Input Hypothesis, (2) the Comprehensible Input Hypothesis, (3) the Interaction Hypothesis, and (4) the Comprehensible Output Hypothesis.

1. The Simplified Input Hypothesis

- Simplified input refers to the language directed at those who have limited proficiency in the language. There are three different types of simplified input: motherese (baby-talk: the talk of mothers, fathers, and other caregivers to babies), teacher talk (the talk of teachers to students, e.g., classroom English), and foreigner talk (the talk of native speakers to non-native speakers). The simplified input hypothesis holds that simplified input provides a rich source of learner intake. This hypothesis was popular among researchers in the early 1980s.

- However, many researchers criticized this hypothesis and argued that simplified input can provide some learners (learners at beginning stages) with good language assistance but that it is not sufficient for language development. Krashen (1980) stated that "with simplified input alone, learners may never reach advanced proficiency. They need more diverse forms of input and assistance."

- Examples of teacher talk (Scarcella & Oxford, 1992, p.37):

  (1) (Attracting attention) Look! Look! Look! I want you to sit down here. Sit down here.
  (2) (Checking understanding) Do you understand?
  (3) (Reviewing) Today, we learned color vocabulary. Blue, green, yellow, red, black, white.
  (4) (Specifying topic) Now, we are going to talk about animals. Big animals.

- **Characteristics of simplified input:** Hatch (1983, p.183) provides the characteristics of simplified input as:

  (1) Pronunciation
  ① Fewer reduced vowels and consonants:
  I want an apple. (o)
  I wanna apple. (x)
  ② Slow rate.
  ③ Longer pauses.

  (2) Vocabulary
  ① High frequency words.
  I see the child. (o)
  I see the kid. (x)
  ② Fewer pronouns.
  I see the man. The man is sitting. (o)
  I see the man. He is sitting. (x)

③ Gestures and pictures are used along with vocabulary.

(3) Grammar

① Short utterances.
See big green ball. (o)
I see the big ball that is green. (x)

② Left dislocations of topic.
Friday, Saturday, you have a nice weekend.

③ More repetitions.
Green ball. Green ball. Pretty big green ball.

(4) Discourse

① More requests for clarification.
What? Huh? What do you mean?

② Fewer interruptions.

③ A clear beginning and ending to conversations.
Okay. This is the end of the lesson. Goodbye.

2. The Comprehensible Input Hypothesis

- The weak point of the simplified input hypothesis is that simplified input can only help those who are at the beginning stages of language development.
- In view of this, Krashen (1980) replaced the simplified input hypothesis with the comprehensible input hypothesis. He suggests that the most important factor for language development is not simplified input, but comprehensible input.
- In the simplified input hypothesis, the input is simplified, but it is not tailored to the learner's proficiency level. In the comprehensible input hypothesis, optimal input for language development is that which approximately matches the learner's proficiency level. According to Krashen's theory, some of the optimal input is beyond the learner's level, while some is below his/her proficiency level.
- However, the comprehensible input hypothesis is also limited. One major criticism is that some learners are observed to be able to understand the input far beyond their proficiency levels. Some researchers like Scarcella and Oxford (1992) suspect that the range of input that can facilitate language acquisition is far wider than the language built around the

student's general level of understanding. Scarcella and Oxford say that comprehensible input is necessary, but it is not sufficient for language acquisition. Like simplified input, comprehensible input is just one form of assistance. Learners need more diverse forms of input in order to reach advanced levels of proficiency.

> ◆ **Optimal input:** The level of English which facilitates learning the most. According to Krashen, optimal input covers easy English (below the learner's level) as well as a bit more difficult English (a step beyond the learner's level of proficiency).

3. The Interaction Hypothesis

- According to the interaction hypothesis, learner interaction facilitates language acquisition. This hypothesis emphasizes the dynamic nature of the interaction between learners, their peers, their teachers and others with whom they interact. Long (1985) emphasizes that comprehensible input is the result of modified interaction. In Long's view, the interaction and input are the two major players in the process of acquisition.
- Van Lier (1988) states that when children learn their first language, they do not first learn sounds, words, sentences, and then with this linguistic knowledge interact with the world around them. They interact with the people around them before they are able to utter their first words. Hence, the interactive nature of conversation among speakers facilitates language acquisition the most.

4. The Comprehensible Output Hypothesis

- Comprehensible output refers to the language production which is just one step beyond the learner's current proficiency level. Swain (1985) questioned the comprehensible input hypothesis. She suggested the comprehensible output hypothesis. It states that what is needed for language acquisition is not simply comprehensible input, but comprehensible output as well. Without speaking, learners do not have the chance to test and refine their knowledge of the language. While speaking, they are pushed from processing meaning to processing form, and in that way they acquire the grammar that they will use in communication.

Task 3: Practice

- Simplify the following passage, "The Prince and His Servants," as much as possible, using the guidelines suggested by Hatch (1983).

  (1) Use high frequency words. Control the number of new words.
  (2) Use fewer pronouns.
  (3) Use short sentences.
  (4) Use simple structures.
  (5) Use sentences in present tense form.
  (6) Use active sentences, and direct speech.
  (7) Repeat key information.

The Prince and His Servants

Once there was a beautiful princess. Many princes wanted to marry the princess, but her mother the queen said to them, "I will give you something to do. If you can do it, you can marry the princess; but if you can't do it, you will be killed." None of the princes could do the things that the queen said. So they were all killed. Every month some new prince came, and was killed.

→

There is a princess. The princess is beautiful. Many princes want to marry the princess. The princess's mother says, "Do something. If you do it, you can marry the princess. ________________________________

____

Task 4: Application

1. Which hypothesis do you think will be the most valuable in your teaching context? Why?

2. Let's look at the activity below. Do you like it? Revise it if you don't like it. Make sure you change it so that it reflects your favored hypothesis.

Ss: Who is he? (looking at a picture of a two-year old boy; it's Minsu's old picture.)
S1: He is Minsu.
Minsu: That's right.
Ss: Who is she?
S1: She is Kisuk.
Kisuk: No, she isn't.

Ss: Who is she?
Kisuk: She is Minkyung.
Minkyung: You are right.

Summary

In this chapter, we have considered:

- ***Learning styles.*** Students use different learning styles to learn a new language. Some learn best through song, others through reading and others through making things. The major language learning styles are analytic-global styles, intuition-sensory styles, sensory preference (visual, auditory, hands-on styles), and closure-open styles.
- ***Language acquisition hypotheses.*** As to language acquisition, there are four major hypotheses: the simplified input hypothesis, the comprehensible input hypothesis, the interaction hypothesis, and the comprehensible output hypothesis. These hypotheses or theories are concerned with the question, "How can we best help our learners learn a new language?"
- **The simplified input hypothesis** holds that simplified input (e.g., easy, simple and clear English) provides a rich source of successful language learning. In the comprehensible input hypothesis, optimal input for language development is the level of language which approximately matches the learner's proficiency level. According to this theory, some of the optimal input is beyond the learner's level, while some is below his/her proficiency level. **The interaction hypothesis** emphasizes the dynamic nature of the interaction between learners, their peers, their teachers and many others. The scholars who support this theory think that the interactive nature of conversation among speakers facilitates language acquisition. In **the comprehensible output hypothesis,** it is argued that learners need not only comprehensible input but also comprehensible output.

Useful Internet Sites

1. Learning styles
   - http://www.chaminade.org/inspire/learnstl.htm
   - http://www.funderstanding.com/learning_styles.cfm
   - http://www.ldpride.net/learningstyles.MI.htm
2. Multiple intelligence
   - http://www.ldpride.net/learningstyles.MI.htm
3. Teaching styles
   - http://homepage.ntlworld.com/vivian.c/SLA/Background%20to%20Language%20Teaching.htm

References and Additional Resources

Dornyei, Z. (1995). On the teachability of communication strategies. *TESOL Quarterly 29,* 55-84.

Hatch, E. (1983). *Psycholinguistics: A second language perspective.* Rowley, MA: Newbury House.

Krashen, S. D. (1980). The theoretical and practical relevance of simple codes in second language acquisition. In R. Scarcella & S. D. Krashen (Eds.), *Research in second language acquisition.* Rowley, MA: Newbury House.

Long, M. H. (1985). Input and second language acquisition theory. In S. M. Gass and C. G. Madden (Eds.), *Input in second language acquisition* (377-393), Rowley, MA: Newbury House.

Scarcella, R. C., & Oxford, R. L. (1992). *The tapestry of language learning.* Boston: Heinle & Heinle Publishers.

Swain, M. (1985). Communicative competence: Some roles of comprehensible input and comprehensible output in its development. In S. M. Gass & C. G. Madden (Eds.), *Input in second language acquisition* (235-253), Rowley, MA: Newbury House.

Van Lier, L. A. W. (1988). *The classroom and the language learner.* London: Longman.

Chapter 5
Vocabulary

Chapter Five presents the importance of teaching vocabulary. Basic teaching steps for vocabulary lessons are also introduced. In addition, several teaching techniques and strategies for vocabulary instruction are given to enhance the student's ability to understand meaning and to remember vocabulary. The tasks added in this chapter will help you apply theoretical knowledge to your teaching in a practical way.

In this chapter, we will consider:
(1) Why is teaching vocabulary important?
(2) What are the major steps in teaching vocabulary?
(3) What techniques help children remember vocabulary?

Teaching Vocabulary

- Vocabulary is a powerful carrier of meaning. Beginning EFL learners often manage to communicate in English by listing words. Children, recognizing the communicative power of vocabulary, tend to focus on learning words at the beginning stage. Hence English teachers need to have a good knowledge of the best way to teach vocabulary to children (Scrivener, 1994).
- Teaching vocabulary was neglected during the 1950s and 1960s when audio-lingualism was a dominant influence on language

teaching methodology. Vocabulary instruction made something of a comeback during the 1970s under the influence of communicative language teaching (Nunan, 1998).

- Researchers (Rivers, 1983; Krashen & Terrel, 1983) have emphasized the importance of vocabulary in teaching ESL:

  (1) During the early stages of learning, EFL students are better served by teachers who focus on vocabulary rather than grammar, and students can communicate better if they have a reasonable vocabulary base.
  (2) Acquisition of an adequate vocabulary is essential for successful language learning because, without an extensive vocabulary, students will be unable to communicate using the structures and functions they are learning.

What Do We Know about Teaching Vocabulary?

1. Vocabulary Acquisition

- Development of a rich vocabulary is an important element in the acquisition of a new language. A new vocabulary item is acquired when the child can identify its meaning in and out of context and use it naturally and appropriately. In other words, children can be said to acquire a new word when they have both productive as well as receptive control of the new word (Channell, 1988).
- **Productive vs. Receptive**: Teachers often make a distinction between productive (or active) and receptive (or passive) vocabulary. Receptive vocabulary refers to the words which children can understand but cannot easily produce in their speech and writing. Productive vocabulary refers to the words that children can use automatically in their speech and writing. Hence a person's acquisition of a word can be placed on a scale running from recognition of the word at one end to its automatic production at the other end:

  Receptive ←——————→ Productive

2. Steps in Teaching Vocabulary

- Many classroom activities are related to reading and listening skills. By reading books and listening to dialogues children learn most of their vocabulary unconsciously (*indirect teaching*). They may also practice and learn parts of their vocabulary by performing specifically designed activities (*direct teaching*). A brief procedure for teaching a vocabulary lesson (direct teaching) is:

  (1) The teacher presents new words using pictures and objects.
  (2) Students practice the words in spoken form.
  (3) The teacher presents the words in written form.
  (4) Students practice the words in written form.
  (5) Students play reading and writing games which involve the new words.
  (6) Follow up (e.g., reading a story which repeatedly uses the new words).

Task 1: Reflect

1. Look at the activity and think about the procedure for teaching the words.

2. Most children in Korea use English words like *cowboy* and *phone* without being taught. Find other words children learn naturally and answer this question.

   - How and why do you think children learn the words so easily?

Vocabulary Teaching in Practice

1. Techniques for Teaching Vocabulary

- **Context clues**: Techniques for guessing the meaning of a new word in context include activating one's background knowledge about the topic of a text, finding clues from grammatical structures, pronunciation, and punctuation in the text. Here is an example.

> ◆ Read these sentences and guess the meaning of "bakery".
> There is a bakery in my neighborhood. I go there to buy bread everyday.

- **Word morphology**: As seen in the examples below, children can increase their vocabulary by combining word stems and by adding affixes.
  bus + stop = bus stop,
  blue + berry = blueberry,
  un + happy = unhappy,
  quiet + ly = quietly

- **Loci**: This is a memory aid in which the words to be learned are associated with a familiar place such as a room, a zoo, or a town. Each word is associated in some way with the place, and the visual image of the place is used to help children recall the words. The learning steps in loci are:

(1) Children imagine (or draw) a familiar place.
(2) They place the first word to be remembered at a certain location, the second word at another location, and so forth.
(3) To recall the words, the children take an imaginary walk along the landmarks in the place and retrieve the words that were "put" there.

- **TPR**: In this technique, target vocabulary items are paired with relevant physical actions. Physically enacting the information (a word or a sentence) facilitates children's recall of the word.
- **Word families**: This is a kind of grouping technique. Exercises, which show a relationship between certain groups of words, can be done to develop "word families." Here are examples.

  Grouping: bowl, cup, fork, knife, dish, spoon,
  Finding: Which word is different from the others?
  1. road, river, street, avenue
  2. book, magazine, TV, letter

  Rhyming: brown, clown, crow

- **Mapping**: Teachers ask children to arrange a set of words into a diagram with a key word and the other words linked to the key word as:

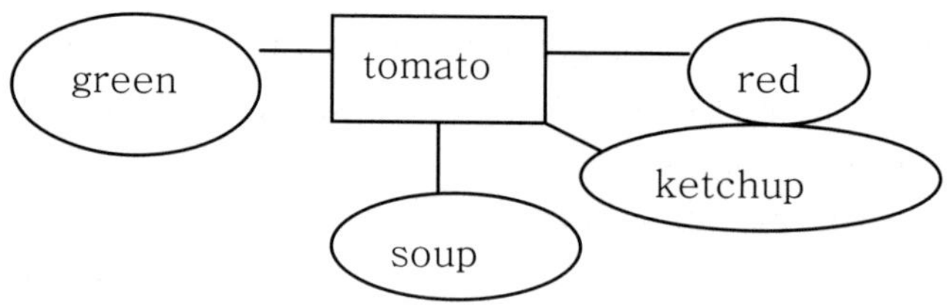

- **Collocation**: Collocations are the words that are commonly associated with each other:

◆ Choose the items that go together.

1. go · · your teeth
2. brush · · shopping
3. read · · books

Examples range from two word combinations such as *problem child* to extended combinations such as *No problem with me* (Lewis, 2000).

- **Visualization**: Children can learn words better by matching words and pictures. Studies have shown that in this way children learn new words faster and more accurately.

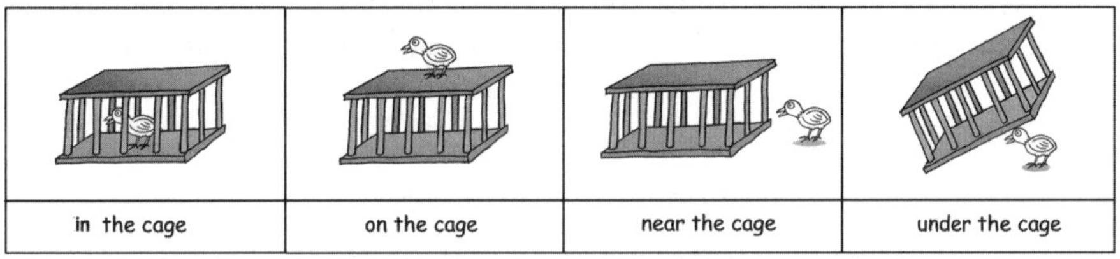

2. Remembering Words

- There is no point in studying new words if they are not remembered. Many children record newly learned words in their notebooks. In many cases these written words are disorganized and are never looked at again (Scrivener, 1994). To memorize and remember words more efficiently children need to put into use some learning aids such as vocabulary notebooks, word-networks and word cards.
- **Vocabulary notebooks**: When children have a special notebook for vocabulary, these notebooks help them pick up new words and strengthen their knowledge of existing ones. Children write down new words in their notebooks during a lesson and review them whenever they are directed to do so.
- **Word networks**: Another strategy reported as useful to children is to make a word network about a particular word (e.g., face). This can form another section in the vocabulary notebook. It is helpful especially when

the learning activities are topic-based. Here is an example (the topic is "a face").

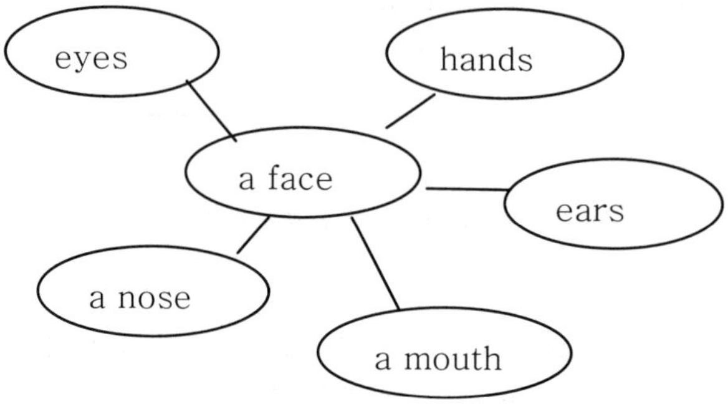

- **Word cards**: As a strategy for keeping words in mind, children can make and use word cards. They can use their cards repeatedly to recall the words and share with each other in pair work - explaining words and information needed. The figure presented below shows a sample word card.

happy	Today is my birthday. I get a lot of presents from my friends. So I'm very happy.
뜻	행복한
반대말	unhappy
강세	h**a**ppy
그림	 He is very happy.

Task 2: Discuss

1. Observe a reading lesson and make notes on the following:

   (1) Did the teacher have any specific aims for teaching vocabulary?
   (2) Was the vocabulary taught explicitly?
   (3) How was the new vocabulary presented?
   (4) What procedures were used to practice the new vocabulary?
   (5) How much responsibility did the children take in learning the new vocabulary?

2. In order to teach the meaning of the word 'desk,' we may point to a real desk in the classroom instead of showing a picture of a desk. However, pictures might be more convenient for some words. Look at the words below. How will you teach the meaning of these words?

   nose, dress, shoe, blackboard, map, clock, watch, leg, wall

Tips on Teaching Vocabulary

- **Encourage children to read extensively.** Children acquire their L1 vocabulary by reading books attentively. The more books children are exposed to, the better and larger vocabulary they will acquire. Let children read books and pay close attention to the words they don't know. Encourage them to guess the meaning of new words in context and then look them up in the dictionary.
- **Let children practice new words a lot.** Studying a word won't help very much if the learner forgets it. Research shows that it takes from 10 to 20 repetitions for a student to really acquire a new word. As soon as children study a new word, help them use it frequently.
- **Let children make as many associations and connections as possible.** Ask children to say a newly learned word aloud to activate their auditory memory; then relate the word to those words they already know.
- **Make children play with words.** Games are a very effective means by which children can practice new words. There are many word games

available for the computer, and children can play games on their computer without a partner.

- **Let children become familiar with the dictionary.** A dictionary is a reliable source for meaning, correct spelling, pronunciation, parts of speech and derivation of words. Teach children how to use a dictionary (a children's dictionary would be better) as early as possible.

Summary

In this chapter, we have considered:

- ***Why is teaching vocabulary important?*** First, children manage to communicate only if they acquire enough vocabulary. Second, a large, rich vocabulary and the skill to use it in communication is the key to successful EFL learning.
- ***What are the steps in teaching vocabulary?*** The typical steps in a vocabulary lesson are: presentation, practice, communicative game, and follow up. This teaching procedure is the same as that used in teaching other skills.
- ***What are the techniques used to help children learn and retain vocabulary?*** The vocabulary-related techniques and activities presented in this chapter are: word morphology, loci, TPR, word families, mapping, collocation, visualization, vocabulary notebooks, vocabulary networks, and word cards.

Useful Internet Sites

1. Web sites for children
    - http://abcteach.com/directory/fun_activities/
    - http://www.edhelper.com/vocabulary.htm

2. Web sites for teachers
    - http://iteslj.org/links/TESL/Articles/Vocabulary/
    - http://teach-nology.com/
    - http://www.lessonplanspage.com/LA23.htm

References and Additional Resources

Channell, J. (1988). Psycholinguistic considerations in the study of L2 vocabulary acquisition. In R. Carter & M. McCarthy (Eds.), *Vocabulary and language teaching*. London: Longman.

Krashen, S., & Terrell, T. (1983). *The natural approach*. Hayward: Alemany Press.

Lewis, M. (2000). *Teaching collocation: Further developments in the lexical approach*. Hove : Language Teaching Publications.

Nunan, D. (1998). *Language teaching methodology*. Hertfordshire: Phoenix ELT.

Pikulski, J. J., & Templeton, S. (2004). Teaching and developing vocabulary: Key to long-term reading success. www.eduplace.com

Rivers, W. M. (1983). *Communicating naturally in a second language*. Cambridge: Cambridge University Press.

Scrivener, J. (1994). *Learning teaching*. Oxford: Macmillan Publishers.

Chapter 6
Pronunciation

Chapter Six presents general information on English pronunciation. It focuses on consonants, vowels and suprasegmentals. It also presents how to organize a pronunciation-focused lesson. The tasks introduce real teaching situations, offering you the chance to use your understanding of English pronunciation to teach English in the classroom.

In this chapter we will consider:
(1) Why did linguists invent a phonetic alphabet for English?
(2) Why are /w/ and /y/ called semi-vowels?
(3) What are suprasegmentals?
(4) What are the main intonation patterns?
(5) What are the main teaching steps in a pronunciation-focused lesson?

General Information

- Children learn pronunciation by imitation. ESL/EFL children mimic native pronunciation quite well. However, in adults who are learning a new language, perfect mimics of pronunciation are very rare (Paulston, 1976).

- As for the optimal age of pronunciation learning, it is well known that before the age of puberty (11-13 years of age) a learner can generally acquire a native pronunciation. Hence, children are more likely to acquire a native English pronunciation when they learn English before puberty.

1. Production of Speech Sounds

- The production of a speech sound is divided into four processes: the initiation of the air stream from the lungs; phonation of a sound in the larynx (through the use of the vocal folds); direction of the sound into the oral or nasal cavity (using the velum); and articulation of a speech sound in the oral cavity (by the tongue).

(1) **The initiation process.** In English, speech sounds are initiated by the movement of an air stream from the lungs. In the initial stage of the production of a speech sound, an air stream moves out of the lungs and goes up the windpipe (trachea).

(2) **The phonation process.** At the upper end of the windpipe, the air stream passes through the larynx. The larynx is a small quantity of cartilage which has vocal folds (vocal cords) and the Adam 's Apple. The gap between the vocal folds are called glottis. The speaker manipulates his vocal folds and changes the shape of the glottis. For example, the narrow glottis (vibration of the vocal folds) produces voiced sounds of speech; the open glottis (non-vibration of the vocal folds) produces voiceless sounds.

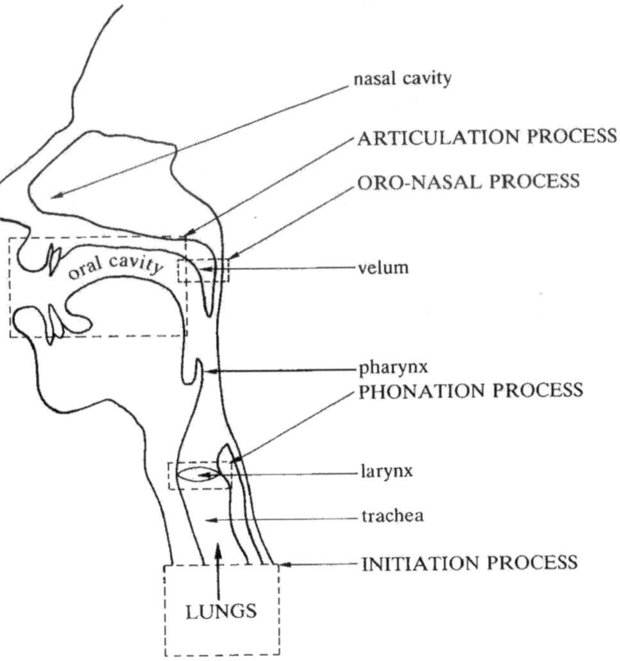

Figure 1. The organs of speech (Giegerich, 1992)

(3) **The oro-nasal process.** After passing through the larynx and the pharynx (the back of the throat), the air stream goes either into the nasal cavity or into the oral cavity. The velum, a soft flap of muscle and tissue in the back of the roof of the mouth, controls this. Raised velum produces oral sounds ([v], [f], [l]), and lowered velum produces nasal sounds ([m], [n]).

(4) **The articulation process.** Speech sounds are articulated in the mouth. Use of the lips and the tongue, and the size and shape of the oral cavity create different speech sounds. In general, speech sounds are distinct from one another depending on their place of articulation and manner of articulation.

2. Segmentals (Phonemes)

- Learning English pronunciation includes good control over the segmental phonemes (consonants, vowels) and the suprasegmental elements (stress, intonation, linking, rhythm).
- A phoneme is the smallest unit of sound in a language (e.g., */p/*) and causes distinct meaning (e.g., *pin*). The words *pin* and *bin* mean different things in English (i.e., each of them has distinctive meaning), and /p/ and /b/ are separate phonemes. Sets of words, which are distinguished by only one phoneme, are called minimal pairs (e.g., pin-bin).
- The English spelling system does not represent all of the English sounds. That is why linguists invented various phonetic symbols (i.e., phonemes) in which one symbol represents one specific sound. English speech sounds are represented in phonetic symbols rather than in letters of the alphabet.
- These basic phonetic symbols are from those of the International Phonetic Association (Edwards, 2003):

Table 1. List of Phonetic Symbols

/p/	*as in*	paper	/j/	*as in*	yellow
/b/		bat	/r/		red
/t/		tape	/i/		eat
/d/		date	/ɪ/		it
/k/		kite	/e/		eight
/g/		go	/ɛ/		head
/f/		fish	/æ/		had
/v/		vent	/ʌ/		hut
/θ/		thin	/ə/		*a*bove
/ð/		then	/ɜ/		herd
/s/		sent	/ɚ/		herd*er*
/z/		Zen	/u/		hoot
/ʃ/		shirt	/ʊ/		hood
/ʒ/		mea*s*ure	/o/		hoe
/h/		hat	/ɔ/		haul
/tʃ/		chip	/ɑ/		hot
/dʒ/		gyp	/ɒ/		hot
/m/		man	/a͜ɪ/		high
/n/		needle	/a͜ʊ/		how
/ŋ/		so*ng*	/ɔ͜ɪ/		toy
/l/		light	/j͜u/		you
/w/		wind			

1) Consonants

- The English consonant phonemes are grouped into several categories according to the place and the manner of their articulations as:

Table 2. The English Consonant Phonemes

(M: Manner of articulation, P: Point of articulation, +: Voiced, −: Voiceless)

P / M	Labial	Labio-dental	Dental	Alveolar	Palatal	Velar	Glottal
Stops	p (−) b (+)			t (−) d (+)		k (−) g (+)	
Fricatives		f (−) v (+)	θ (−) ð (+)	s (−) z (+)	ʃ(−) ʒ(+)		h
Affricates					tʃ (−) dʒ (+)		
Nasals	m			n		ŋ	
Liquids				1, r			
Glides	w				y		

(1) **Stops**: *p(pin), b(bin), t(tin), d(din), k(kin), g(gun).* The stream of air is cut off completely at some point in the vocal tract, and is released completely.

(2) **Fricatives**: *f(fan), v(van), θ(thin), ð(then). s(sue), z(zoo), ʃ(shine), ʒ (measure), h(hunt).* The stream of air is impeded, but not cut off completely. Then it is released.

(3) **Affricates**: tʃ*(chair), dʒ(jar).* The stream of air is first stopped and then released as in fricatives.

(4) **Nasals**: *m(me), n(no), ŋ(ring).* The air passes through the nasal cavity.

(5) **Liquids**: *r(red), l(lead).* The passage of air is obstructed in the middle of the mouth, and air escapes around the sides of the tongue.

(6) **Glides**: *w(wet), y(yes).* There is very little restriction with these sounds. They are called semi-vowels.

2) Vowels

a. The chart below shows the main English vowels and the position of the tongue and jaw for their pronunciation (Paulston, 1976).

Table 2. The English Vowel Phonemes

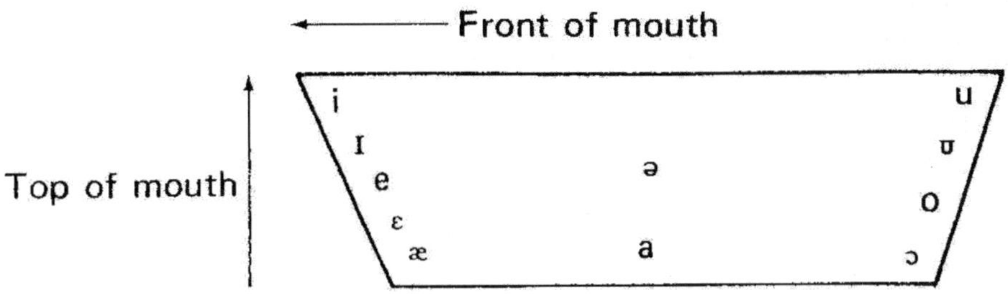

Phoneme	*Example*
i	peel, Pete
ɪ	pill, pit
e	pail, pate
ɛ	pell (as pell mell), pet
æ	pal, pat
a	pot
ə	putt
ɔ	Paul
o	pole
ʊ	pull
u	pool
Diphthongs	
aɪ	pie
ɔɪ	poise
aʊ	pout

Task 1: Practice (Phonemes)

- Say these sentences, and describe your and your friend's pronunciation in phonetic symbols.

1. Hans had a beautiful gold ring.
   Yours: ______________________________
   Your friend's: ______________________________

2. Do you want this nice ring?
   Yours: ______________________________
   Your friend's: ______________________________

3. They took Hans away.
   Yours: ______________________________
   Your friend's: ______________________________

4. She shut him in a room.
   Yours: ______________________________
   Your friend's : ______________________________

3. Suprasegmentals

- Suprasegmental phonemes are stress, rhythm, and intonation. They are called suprasegmentals, because they occur with segmentals (vowels and consonants) and are overlaid on the segmentals.

1) Stress

- Stress is "the degree of force with which a sound or syllable is uttered (Jones, 1976)," or simply "the degree of loudness." It is the activity of speaking one of the syllables in a word louder than the remaining syllables.
- English is a "free stress" language. The stress can occur on any syllable. There are four levels of stress for sentences as in the following example:

4 2 1 4 3
A *big* **birth**day<u>cake</u> (1:primary, *2*: secondary, <u>3</u>: tertiary, 4: unstressed)

- **Teaching stress**. The first stage is imitation; a repetition of the model pronunciation in chorus or individually. For example, in "Good morning," the teacher repeats the whole phrase, then he isolates the stressed syllable - MOR -, repeats it several times, and then repeats the whole phrase again. So the process is as follows:

  ① Repeat whole phrase. (Good morning)
  ② Isolate and repeat stressed syllable only. (Mor-)
  ③ Repeat whole phrase. (Good morning)

- The teacher may indicate the position of the stressed syllable by gestures. He may thump the air when saying the stressed syllable, or make a downward stroke of the hand.

2) **Rhythm (sentence stress)**

- Rhythm involves some noticeable event happening at regular intervals of time (Roach, 1991). Rhythm can be found in the internal activity of our body. For example, the beat of the heart has a heavy movement and a light movement: the two movements alternate regularly and form rhythm. The same is true of the English language. Stressed syllables occur at relatively regular intervals and form rhythm.
- Pike (1945) distinguished two types of speech rhythm: syllable-timed rhythm, in which the syllables come at equal intervals in time, and stress-timed rhythm, in which the stressed syllables occur at regular intervals. While syllable-timed rhythm is compared to the rhythm of a machine gun, stress-timed rhythm is compared to that of Morse code. French, Spanish, Italian, Korean and Japanese belong to the former types; English and Russian belong to the latter.
- In English, the stressed syllables tend to occur at regular intervals, and the unstressed syllables are reduced and given less time.

●	●	●
Class	**starts**	**now** (3 syllables).
●	●	●
The **class**	is **star**ting	to**day** (7 syllables).
●	●	●
The **class**	should be **star**ting	to**mor**row (10 syllables).

- In these example sentences, despite the difference in the number of syllables, the actual time between the stresses would be almost the same. Thus all the unstressed syllables are put together and reduced, producing almost the same pattern of rhythm.
- In informal speech, the unstressed vowels are often reduced to a mid-vowel, such as /ə/. In the following sentence, the underlined syllables are all pronounced /ə/. This phenomenon makes comprehension very difficult, because the sound has little relation to the written representation of the sentence.

He wants *a* c*ou*ple *of* apples.

- In general, content words are stressed and function words are unstressed. **Function words** are **closed class** words (only about 300 in English) while **content words** are **open class** words (new words are being added in every language).

Function Words	Examples
Prepositions	*of, at, in, without, between*
Pronouns	*he, they, anybody, it, one*
Determiners	*the, a, that, my, more, much, either, neither*
Conjunctions	*and, that, when, while, although, or*
Modal verbs	*can, must, will, should, ought, need, used*
Auxiliary verbs	*be (is, am, are), have, got, do*
Particles	*no, not, nor, as*

Content Words	Examples
Nouns	*John, room, answer, Selby*
Adjectives	*happy, new, large, gray*
Full verbs	*search, grow, hold, have*

Adverbs	*really, completely, very, also, enough*
Numerals	*one, thousand, first*
Interjections	*eh, ugh, phew, well*
Yes/No answers	*yes, no* (as answers)

- The same lexical word can function as either a *content* or *function* word depending on its use in an utterance.

  I <u>have</u> come to see you. (function word)
  I <u>have</u> three apples. (content word)
  I have <u>no</u> money (function word)
  <u>No</u>, I am not coming. (content word)

Task 2: Practice (Stress)

1. Mark the stressed words in these sentences, and say them.

   (1) I saw your brother yesterday.
   (2) Can I carry your suitcase?
   (3) Would you like a glass of milk?
   (4) Have you heard about John?
   (5) He's going to New York tomorrow.
   (6) My wife's waiting for me at the corner of the street.

2. This is the story "Little Red Hen." Mark the stressed syllables and read it.

Little Red Hen

"Will you help me plant the wheat?" asked Little Red Hen.
"No," said the rat, the cat and the dog.
"Then I will plant it all by myself," said Little Red Hen. And she did.

"Will you help me cut the wheat?" asked Little Red Hen.
"No," said the rat, the cat and the dog.
"Then I will cut it all by myself," said Little Red Hen. And she did.

"Will you help me make the flour?" asked Little Red Hen.
"No," said the rat, the cat and the dog.
"Then I will make it all by myself," said Little Red Hen. And she did.

"Will you help me make the bread?" asked Little Red Hen.
"No," said the rat, the cat and the dog.
"Then I will make it all by myself," said Little Red Hen. And she did.

"Will you help me eat the bread?" asked Little Red Hen.
"Yes," said the rat, the cat and the dog.
"No," said Little Red Hen. "I will eat it all by myself." And she did!

3) Intonation

- Intonation is the rise and fall in the pitch of the voice as we speak. It is sometimes illustrated as notes on a musical scale. The three pitch levels are very common in English:

  3 high
  2 normal
  1 low

- The pitch at the end of an utterance is also characteristic. There are two main types: rising and falling. In English, intonation is related to sentence stress, since the accented syllables are often spoken on a high note. The most common intonation patterns are /231↓/ and /233↑/.

(1) **/231↓/:** This pattern is used for declarative sentences, requests, commands, and WH questions.

I'm going downtown.

I'm going downtown tomorrow.

Where is he going?

(2) **/233↑/:** This pattern is used for yes-no questions, questions with statement word order.

Are you going?

You are not ready?

It's time for class?

4) Linking

- In English, words are often linked together and are pronounced as if they were one word. When a word ends with a consonant, and it is followed by a word which begins with a vowel or the same consonant, the two words are linked together as if they were one word.

Task 3: Practice (Linking)

1. Practice the following sentences.

   (1) He likes apples.
   (2) She wants an eraser.
   (3) Tom and Jim are friends.
   (4) We're running in the same race tomorrow.
   (5) She's singing well.
   (6) Fred doesn't like tea.
   (7) I'd decided before I met Mary.

2. Turn back to the story of "Little Red Hen." Mark the intonation and linking.

Tips on Teaching Pronunciation

- Learn how to describe pronunciation. Familiarize yourself with the phonemic symbols for English, and with a system for describing basic intonation patterns. This knowledge will help you to understand the language problems of your students. For example, English has a large number of consonant clusters (e.g., straight, strawberries, glue, black). They cause problems for children, because these combinations do not occur in Korean. Knowledge of these English consonant clusters can change and improve your lessons (Wharton & Race, 1999).
- Record your students' speech. Listen to the recordings of your students and see where their difficulties lie. Think about which of their difficulties is most significant.
- Be aware of your own pronunciation. Your accent may be different from the standard pronunciation model. Tell your students there is more than one acceptable model.
- Teach pronunciation a little at a time. Pronunciation will improve as the students do lots of listening and speaking. Frequent, short pronunciation practices are the most useful.
- Let students listen to their recordings of themselves. This can be a valuable pronunciation learning strategy. Students may consciously notice weak areas and try to correct their pronunciation.

- Teach some phonemic symbols. This can be done selectively and gradually. Once students know the symbols, you have a very useful means to talk about pronunciation. For most learners, the /θ/ and /ð/ pair is difficult, because these sounds are absent in Korean. Identifying these sounds may be of great help.

  this that there think thing

Steps in a Pronunciation Lesson

- The basic steps in a pronunciation lesson are the same as in the procedure of other lessons. They are presentation, recognition and production.

1. Presentation

- The first step in a pronunciation lesson is to introduce a sound (or sounds), and to focus the student's attention on the sound features you wish to teach. In this step, a native model pronunciation is necessary. The teacher also can use gestures and graphic symbols. For example, the teacher can raise or lower his hand at the end of the model sentence to teach a certain intonation pattern (e.g., Are you hungry? What do you want?).

2. Aural Recognition

1) Same-different exercise
   - The purpose of this exercise is to make sure the students can hear the phonemic contrasts. The teacher pronounces pairs of words (e.g., pin/bin) and the students are asked to identify whether the sounds are same or different.

     (1) T: 1 cat, 2 cap, 3 cat
         S: 1 and 3.
     (2) T: I like this cat. I like this cap.
         S: Different.

2) True-false exercise

- In the following exercise, the teacher says a sentence, and the students are asked to identify whether the sentence is true or false.

T: The cat is running after a mouse. S: True.
T: The cap is running after a mouse. S: False

3) Discriminating exercise

- In this type of exercise, the students are asked to discriminate between grammatical patterns they are learning. For example, while they are learning the yes-no questions, the students are required to discriminate between the sentences.

T: The cat is running. S: Statement.
T: The cat is running? S: Question.

3. Production

- Once the students can identify a new sound, they must learn to produce it. They produce the new sound first in words, then in phrases, later in sentences, and finally in communicative utterances.

1) Repetition drills

- The teacher reads the words; the students repeat them as a group and then individually.

T: cat, cap, cat S: cat, cap, cat

2) Frame drills

- The teacher gives a sentence frame, and the students complete it using given words.

(1) It's my ______________.
cat, cap
(2) Do your have a ______ ?
cat, cap

3) Chain drills

- Memory chain drills can be used for many purposes. A chain drill for practicing -s endings is:

S1: My name is Minsu. I like cats.
S2: His name is Minsu. He likes cats. My name is Insuk. I like dogs.
S3: His name is Minsu. He likes cats. Her name is Insuk. She likes dogs. My name is Kisu. I like monkeys.

4) Chants

- For practicing rhythm, stress, and intonation, chants are very useful. They can be personalized to fit the students in the class. For example:

What's your name and/ what do you like?
What's your name and/ what do you like?
My name is Miran and/ I like cats.
My name is Miran and/ I like cats.
What's your name and/ where're you from?
What's your name and/ where're you from?
My name is Kisu and/ I'm from Bosung.
My name is Kisu and/ I'm from Bosung.

5) Dictation

- It is also possible to use a dictation with gaps as a means of making students aware of some speech sounds. In this dialog, the underlined words are omitted from the student text and must be filled in.

A: Did you see Tom today?
B: No, I didn't.
A: Where did he go?
B: I don't know.

6) Roleplay

- In the production stage, we can use dialogues for roleplay. For example:

Boy: Ready?
Girl: No.
Boy: Why?
Girl: Problems.
Boy: Problems?
Girl: Yes.
Boy: What?
Girl: Money.

Task 4: Application

- Here are some sample activities that focus on pronunciation. Plan each activity using the three-step teaching procedure introduced in this chapter.

1. Ask and answer

A: What's this/that? /th/
B: It's a monkey/an apple/a dog/a bench.

2. Look and Say

 chalk	 ship
 chair	 shopkeeper
 teacher	 shop

Summary

In this chapter we have considered:

- ***The English phonetic symbols.*** The English spelling system does not represent all of the English sounds. That is why linguists invented various phonetic symbols called phonemes in which each symbol represents a specific sound.
- ***Suprasegmentals.*** Suprasegmentals are stress, rhythm, and intonation. They are called suprasegmentals, because they occur with segmentals (consonants and vowels) and they are overlaid on the segmentals.
- ***Teaching steps in a pronunciation lesson.*** The basic steps in a pronunciation lesson are almost the same as in the procedure of other lessons. They are presentation, aural recognition and production.

References and Additional Resources

Jones, D. (1976). *An outline of English phonetics.* Cambridge: Cambridge University Press.

Edwards, H. T. (2003). Applied phonetics: The sounds of American English. New York: Delmar Learning.

Giegerich, H. J. (1992). *English phonology: An introduction.* Cambridge: Cambridge University Press.

Paulston, C. B. (1976). *Teaching English as a second language: Techniques and procedures.* Cambridge: Winthrop Publishers.

Pike, K. L. (1945*). The intonation of American English.* University of Michigan Press.

Roach, P. (1991). *English phonetics and phonology.* Cambridge: Cambridge University Press.

Scarcella, R.C., & Oxford, R. L. (1992). *The tapestry of language learning.* Boston: Heinle & Heinle Publishers.

Wharton, S., & Race, P. (1999). *500 tips for TESOL.* London: Koran Page.

Chapter 7
Listening

Chapter Seven presents how to teach listening to children. It introduces the basic types of listening tasks and various listening activities. The tasks given in this chapter will present real teaching situations, offering you the chance to use your understanding to teach a lesson, which focuses on listening.

In this chapter we will consider:
(1) What is listening and why is it important in teaching English?
(2) What are the four stages of listening comprehension?
(3) Why is paying attention important in listening processing?
(4) How can you make listening easier and more interesting for children?

General Information

1. What Is Listening?

- Listening, like reading, is a receptive skill of language. The purpose of listening is to decode the message and reach out to the speaker's meaning.
- Hence, listening is naturally meaning-focused rather than form-focused. For example, children listening to a story in a foreign language will outline the meaning of the story in their minds. Because the story is told in a foreign language they do not fully understand, they will probably try to process the story in their first language, or in mentalese (a mental way of processing meaning).

2. Listening Is Important

- Listening is not an isolated skill. In most daily communication, listening occurs in conjunction with speaking. One person speaks, the other person listens. Only in certain circumstances, such as watching TV and listening to the radio, does listening become an isolated skill.
- Hence oral communication is a two-way process between speaker and listener. It involves the productive skill of speaking and the receptive skill of listening. The diagram below shows how all four skills are related.

	spoken		
receptive	Listening	speaking	productive
	Reading	writing	
	written		

- The reason why listening is important in teaching English to children is that it is the most frequently used skill. Students spend more than half of their school time listening to their teacher and classmates (Scarcella & Oxford, 1992). On the average, we listen twice as much as we speak, four times more than we read, and five times more than we write (Rivers, 1981). Consequently the students' ability to understand needs to be greater than their ability to speak. The diagram below adopted from Byrne (1986) shows that students need a broad receptive base in order to communicate.

PRODUCTIVE
R E C E P T I V E

- Listening skill is important even for L1 children. Recently scholars have been increasingly emphasizing the importance of L1 oral skills (speaking and listening) instruction in school. For a long time, it had been taken for granted that native speakers did not need instruction in how to speak and listen. Also it has been observed that the oral skills of L1 children are better acquired through instruction (Brown, 1984). This indicates that EFL children need special instruction and practice in their listening skill.

3. Aspects of Listening

- Listening involves a number of elements. Included are perception, and four areas of comprehension (word, phrase, sentence, and extended speech). The first task of the beginning listener is to perceive. Perceiving distinguishes the important sounds from an ongoing stream of sounds and finds meaning. This is done by breaking sound up into meaningful units. Perception is followed by these four stages of listening comprehension.

1) Four stages of comprehension

(1) Word recognition within the sound stream. The student can catch a few words, and guess at the meaning of a conversation from them.

(2) Phrase or formula recognition. The learner can recognize some phrases, such as 'Raining, again.' 'Good morning,' 'Hi, how are you?' 'Fine, and you?'.

(3) Clause or sentence recognition. At this stage of comprehension, the student can recognize clauses or sentences that are not routine or formulaic.

(4) Extended speech comprehension. The student can understand a conversation or any general oral communication.

2) Two types of listening processing

- There are two types of processing listening input (Celce-Murcia, 1991). They are bottom-up processing and top-down processing. In bottom-up processing, the listener decodes the sounds in a linear way, from phonemes to words, to phrases, to utterances and texts. Meaning is derived during the last step in this process. Dictation is a good example.
- In top-down processing, on the other hand, the listener reconstructs the speaker's meaning using incoming sounds as cues. In this process, the listener uses his background knowledge and tries to make sense of what he hears. Listening for the main idea is a good example.
- These are examples of top-down and bottom-up listening.

(1) Bottom-up listening

Discriminating between intonation patterns (fall, rise)
Discriminating between phonemes (same, different)
Word/phrase recognition
Clock time recognition

Listen and complete a phone number

(2) Top-down listening
Discriminating between emotions (happy, sad, angry)
Recognizing the topic, location…
Getting the gist of a sentence or a paragraph

4. Language Function and Listening Materials

1) Two types of language function

- Brown and Yule (1983) divide language into two types in terms of function: interactional language and transactional language.

(1) **Interactional language.** The purpose of interactional language is to develop social relationships and express personal attitudes. Interactional language is listener-oriented, and focuses on the person rather than on the information. Some features of interactional language use are:

① Talking about "safe" topics (e.g., weather).
② Shifting of topics with a great deal of agreement among speakers.
③ Expressing opinions.
④ Maintaining "face" and respecting "face."
⑤ Being nice to the other person.
⑥ Being less careful about details.

(2) **Transactional language.** The purpose of transactional language is to deliver factual information. Transactional language is message-oriented, and focuses on the content rather than on the person. Some examples are:

① Instructing
② Giving directions
③ Explaining
④ Describing
⑤ Ordering
⑥ Requesting

2) A model of material design

- Richards (1983) proposes a model of material design for second language listening comprehension. He uses these two language functions and two language processes in his model:

	bottom up	top down
interactional	①	③
transactional	②	④

- In Richard's model, listening materials are divided into these four types: interactional bottom up, transactional bottom up, interactional top down, and transactional top down. Examples are:

  ① Listening closely to a joke
  ② Listening closely to instructions during a first driving lesson
  ③ Listening casually to party "talk"
  ④ Listening casually to air safety instructions

5. Isolating the Skill of Listening

- Activities designed to practice listening generally involve the other skills as well. One way to practice only listening is by asking students to answer to what they hear in non-linguistic ways. Some examples are:

  (1) Students have pictures. They listen and circle the appropriate picture (e.g., *A is tall. But B isn't tall. Put a circle around A.*).

(2) Students have pictures. They listen and number the pictures.

Number 2. It has four legs. It's quite big. You can ride it.
Number 1. It has four legs. It's small. It likes cheese.

(1)

(2)

(3) Students have a map. They listen and name the buildings.

The school is on Main Street. The hospital is on Park Avenue. The zoo is in the park.

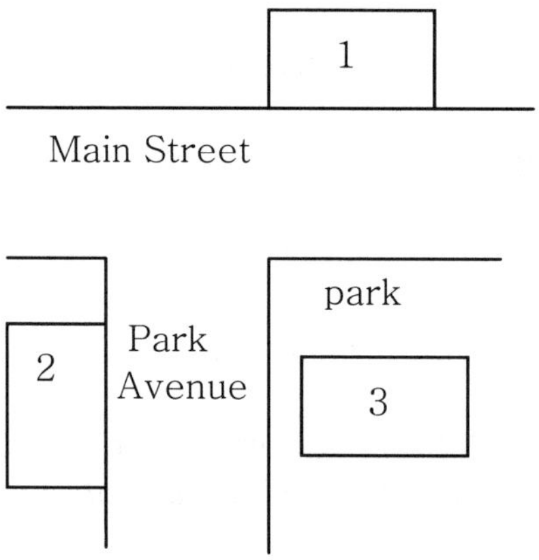

Listening Activities

(Adapted from Cameron, 2001; Olsen, 1977; Shrum & Glisan, 1994; Shoemaker & Shoemaker, 1991).

1. Listen and Do

- In these listen-and-do activities, students listen to the names or characteristics of animals and become familiar with the words by playing games. After playing the games a few times, the children will speak the words as well as listen.
- For example, as the procedure below shows, students play a game with the teacher presenting how to play. Then a student takes over the teacher's role; the other students play as a whole class. Later students play in pairs or groups.

(1) Play as a class (teacher-Ss): presentation
(2) Play as a class (S1-Ss) : presentation/practice
(3) Play in pairs or groups: practice
(4) Play in pairs in front: review

(1) Listen and identify

① The teacher says the name of an object and lets the child point to the picture.
② The teacher makes sure that the pupils understand the spoken word.
③ The teacher describes the picture in more detail for advanced pupils.

T: Dog. It barks, bow-wow. This animal has four legs and barks, wow-wow.
Ss: They point to the picture of a dog.

(2) Bingo

① The teacher gives students 8-10 animal pictures.
② Each student chooses four or six pictures, and puts the other pictures aside.

③ The teacher says the names of the animals at random. When a student hears one of his animals' names, he turns that picture over. The first one with all six pictures turned over shouts "bingo!" and wins the game.

④ The teacher can describe the features of the animals instead of saying the names.

(3) **Listen and take away**

① Students start with a set of pictures (about 10-15 animal pictures).

② The teacher tells them to take away certain pictures.

T: Take away all the animals with wings.
Take away all the animals that live in water.

③ This game goes on until only one picture is left. Anyone who has that picture is the winner.

(4) Find the odd one out

① The students have a set of pictures. The teacher says the names of four animals. The students pick them out and say which is the odd one:

T: dog, cat, lion, fish

Ss: Fish is the odd one. Because it lives in water.

② If the students cannot say the reason why that picture is the odd one, the teacher gives them the sentence. As the game goes on, the students begin to learn the necessary sentences.

(5) Listen and put

① Students draw a cage, a house, and a field on a sheet of paper. They listen and place the animal pictures.

T: The lion lives in the cage.
The cat lives in the house.
The squirrel lives in the field.

② The students can draw a zoo and place the animals as they are told. They can draw the animals instead of using ready-made pictures.

③ At the end of the activity, students can tell a story about their picture.

2. Listen and Say

- In these activities, students say something. The teacher has a set of enlarged pictures, and holds them up for the whole class to see. Students can take over the teacher's role; then play the games in pairs or groups.

(1) Look and choose

① The teacher describes a group of animals.

② Each student chooses one animal and tells what he chooses.

T: Choose an animal with four legs and a tail.
S1: I choose a monkey. It has four legs and a tail.
S2: I choose a bear. It has four legs and a tail.
S3: I choose a tiger. It has four legs and a tail.

(2) Listen and sort

① The teacher names some animals and students pick out the animals' pictures.

② Then the students describe the group of animals, e.g. after picking up tiger, lion, and wolf, they say '*dangerous animals.*'

(3) **Tennis game**

① Students are divided into two groups.
② A student from the first team says the name of an animal and a student from the other team responds with the name of another animal.
③ The game goes on as long as the students can say animal names without repetition.

A: Tiger.
B: Monkey.
A: Lion.
B: Cow.

④ They may say the names of peaceful animals, colors, fruit...

(4) **Guess my animal - questions**

① The teacher chooses an animal but does not tell.
② The students guess by asking *yes/no* questions, e.g. Is it an animal? This activity is good for practicing *yes/no* questions.

(5) **Guess my animal - actions**

① A student chooses an animal and other students tell him to act like the animal.

Sleep like your animal.
Eat like your animal.
Walk like your animal.

② The student who says the name of the animal comes to the front and continues the game.

3. Dictation

- Dictation can take two forms, spot dictation, and the dictation of a complete passage.

(1) **Spot dictation**: The students fill in the blank spaces. This is a sample spot dictation which reviews pronouns. The teacher reads the passage three times.

Tony is tall. (   ) is in the 3rd grade. His homeroom teacher is Miss

Manker. (   ) is tall and kind to her students. He likes (   ).
(Answer: He, She, her)

(2) **Dictation of a complete passage**: The students listen to a passage (or a sentence) three times, and write down what they hear. The procedure is as follows:

① The passage is read at normal speed.
② The passage is read in short word groups with pauses for the students to write.
My name is/ Jane.
I'm in the/ third grade.
I like/ basketball.
③ The passage is reread at normal speed so that the students can check and correct their work.

Often the number of words that the students write is given at the end of each blank.

① ______________________________(6 words)
(The students hear: Mira goes to school at eight.)
② ______________________________(7 words)
(The students hear: She arrives at school at eight thirty.)

(3) **Dictation with repetition**: We can add a repetition phase to dictation exercises like ① listen, ② repeat, and ③ write. The students hear a sentence (or a word), repeat it, hear it again, and then write it.

4. Listening for the Message

- In addition to exercises which focus on specific aspects of grammar, students need practice in listening to whole passages and identifying the main ideas.

(1) **Listen and draw**: The students listen to a description and draw a picture. They can ask the teacher questions. When they finish, they compare their drawings with the one the teacher has. The student whose drawing is the most similar to the teacher's is the winner.

(Example passage)
Today, I want you to draw a picture of a monkey. The monkey is wearing sunglasses. He is holding an umbrella with his left hand. He has a ball near his right foot .

(2) **Listen and check**: The students listen to the conversation and fill in the information sheet.

Tom: What color is your bag, Julie?
Julie: It's blue and white. What about yours?
Tom: Black. But my pencil case is yellow.
Julie: Really? My pencil case is yellow, too.

	bag	pencil case	bike	desk
Tom				
Julie				

Task 1: Reflect

1. Mr. C teaches English at an elementary school. He believes in a teacher-centered classroom in order to control his classes. His teaching plans are grammar-oriented. He feels that knowing a language means understanding grammar rules and vocabulary. Although his command of English is very good, he speaks English only during his presentation of dialogues and while practicing grammar exercises. Since he feels that his students have great difficulty understanding spoken English, he translates everything he says into Korean. He feels that beginning-level students need to learn grammar first and then later apply the rules to meaningful communication.

   1. What do you think the listening process is like for students in Mr. C's class?

   2. If you were Mr. C, what changes would you make for your class?

Task 2: Application

- Look again at the listening activities provided in this chapter. Choose one and design a lesson focused on listening.

Summary

In this chapter we have considered:

- ***What is listening?*** Listening is a receptive skill. Its purpose is to decode the message and reach out to the speaker's meaning. Hence listening is meaning-focused.
- ***Why is listening important?*** Listening is the most frequently used skill. Students spend more than half of their school time listening. They listen twice as much as they speak, four times more than they read, and five times more than they write. That is why listening is important in English classrooms.
- ***What are the four stages of listening comprehension?*** Students go through four stages of comprehension when they learn to listen in a new language. They are: word recognition, phrase recognition, sentence recognition, and extended speech comprehension.
- ***What are the two types of listening processing?*** They are bottom-up processing and top-down processing.

Useful Internet Sites

1. http://www.esl-lab.com
2. http://oyez.at.nwu.eu/oyez.html
3. http://www.webcorp.com
4. http://www.realaudio.com

References and Additional Resources

Brown, H. D. (1984). *Principles of language learning and teaching.* Englewood Cliffs, NJ: Prentice-Hall.

Brown, G., and Yule, G. (1983). *Discourse analysis.* Cambridge: Cambridge University Press.

Byrne, D. (1986). *Teaching oral English.* London: Longman.

Cameron, L. (2001). *Teaching languages to young learners.* Cambridge: Cambridge University Press.

Celce-Murcia, M. (Ed.) (1991). *Teaching English as a second or foreign language.* New York: Newbury House.

Olsen, J. W. (1977). *Communication starters.* Hayward, CA: Alemany Press.

Richards, J. C. (1983). Listening comprehension: Approach, design, procedure. *TESOL Quarterly, 17,* 219-239.

Scarcella, R., & Oxford, R. (1992). *The tapestry of language learning.* Florence: Heinle & Heinle Publishers.

Shrum, J. L., & Glisan, E. W. (1994). *Teacher's handbook.* Boston: Heinle and Heinle Publishers.

Shoemaker, C. L., & Shoemaker, F. F. (1991). *Interactive techniques for the ESL classroom.* New York: Newbury House.

Chapter 8
Speaking

Chapter Eight presents speaking proficiency and its major components. The "3P teaching cycle (presentation, practice, production) has been presented as a guiding principle for teaching oral skills. The tasks given in this chapter will provide you with the chance to use your theoretical knowledge to teach a lesson, which focuses on speaking.

In this chapter we will consider:
(1) What constitutes speaking proficiency?
(2) How is controlled practice different from guided practice?
(3) How will you introduce a new language to children?

Successful English Learners

- Several decades ago when the grammar-translation method was dominant in teaching languages, the accuracy of the language produced was the major criterion used to judge a student's success. During that period, students knew a good deal about the language, but they were unable to use that knowledge to communicate appropriately.

- However, development in English language teaching has moved us from a focus on accurate form to a focus on communicative effectiveness (Riggenbach and Lazaraton, 1991). Today students are considered successful if they can communicate well in English. This means that successful students are required not only to have a good knowledge of English, but also to know how to put that knowledge into active use.
- These days communicative competence is considered the ultimate goal of language teaching. What is communicative competence? We assume most ordinary native speakers are competent and are able to communicate in

their first language, i.e., they have communicative competence. In this sense, communicative competence refers to the ability of native speakers to communicate in their mother tongue.

- Communicative competence has four major skill areas, i.e., listening, speaking, reading and writing. Apart from the four language skills, educators and researchers (Canale & Swain, 1980) have recognized that "communicative competence" includes not only grammatical accuracy but also knowledge in other areas. In chapter 3, it was mentioned that communicative competence includes grammatical competence, sociolinguistic competence, discourse competence, and strategic competence. Speaking proficiency means oral communicative competence. Hence, an effective speaker is competent in these four areas.

Factors Affecting the Development of Speaking Proficiency

- Considering the major competences, it is obvious that learners need activities and exercises which promote communicative competence. Several factors affect the development of speaking proficiency. These include the number of chances the learner has a) to interact with native speakers, b) to participate in fluency and accuracy activities and c) to participate in strategic training.

1. More Chances to Interact

- Students need to participate in many different communicative situations. They also need interaction with a variety of speakers. The more opportunities to interact with proficient English speakers they have, the greater chance they have of developing their speaking proficiency.
- Cooperative learning (Shrum & Glisan, 1994) in which students work in pairs or in small groups to do a given task can increase the amount of meaningful interaction.
- These are guidelines for structuring group work (Shrum & Glisan, 1994):

  (1) Limit the size of the group. Groups are most effective when there are no more than five participants.
  (2) Motivate the activity with actions, visuals, videos, or drama.

(3) Set clear goals and describe the outcome clearly for the students.
(4) Provide the language students need to do the activity.
(5) Give directions and a model.
(6) Set a time limit to help the students make the best use of the time available.
(7) Circulate among the students, offer assistance and check progress.
(8) Elicit feedback at the end of the activity.

2. Fluency and Accuracy Activities

- Many educators believe that students should practice their speaking skill through communicative tasks and activities. They believe fluency is important when teaching English for communication. They are against focusing on accuracy during these activities. However, fluency cannot be developed by simply providing students with lots of conversation practice. They need both types of activities. Through fluency activities (which are related to discourse, sociolinguistic and strategic competence), students practice what they already know. Through accuracy activities (which are related to grammatical competence), they perfect their mastery of the target language.

3. Strategy Training

- We can teach students how to ask for clarification (What?), how to ask others to repeat (What did you say?) or how to ask others to slow down (Can you speak more slowly?), etc. We can also teach them how to look interested and to keep the conversation going (That's funny!). These tools enable students to participate and interact from the very beginning stage of learning.

The "3P" Teaching Cycle

- How do we teach speaking to children? The 3P teaching format is dominant in many parts of the world. It has three stages: presentation, practice and production. At the presentation stage, the teacher introduces new language items or textbook materials to students. At the practice stage, the students practice the introduced language through a series of drills. At the final stage, the students use the language for communication in a series of communicative tasks.

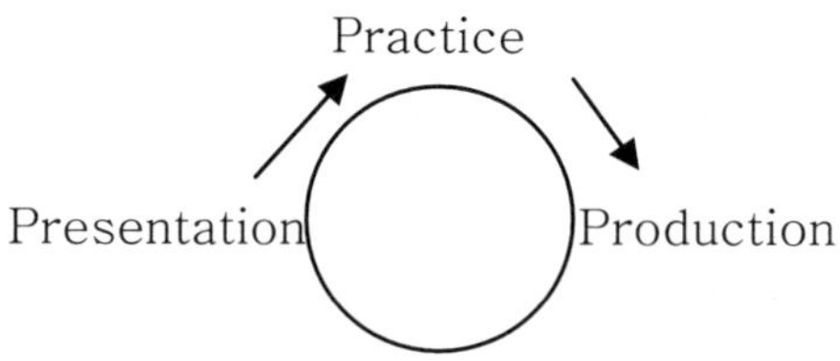

- Nunan (1999) illustrates the main characteristics of each stage in Table 1. In Nunan's view, students should be given as many chances as possible to practice the target language in meaningful situations. Sufficient opportunities to use the language are crucial for the students' language development.

Table 1. The 3P Teaching Cycle (adapted from Nunan, 1999)

	Presentation	Practice	Production
Role of teacher	model	monitor	conductor
Role of student	listener	performer	interactor
Type of activity	lecture	drill	roleplay
Class organization	whole class	pairs	small groups

1. How to Present New Language Orally

- Children need to be given language before they can produce it. Language must go in before it can come out. Here are some ways, suggested by Scott & Ytreberg (1990), through which the teacher can present new language orally.

1) Through the pupils

- The teacher can present new language orally through the students. In this case, the teacher should know about his/her students well. So he/she says, "Mina can play the piano. Inyoung can play the violin. Jisuk can play soccer. Cholhyun can swim." These sentences should be true and accompanied with appropriate actions and sounds.

2) **Using a mascot**

- One of the most effective ways of presenting new language is through puppets or a class mascot. For example, if you use Hodori as your mascot, you can present dialogs with Hodori as your partner. For example:

T: Hodori, can you swim?
H: Yes, I can.
T: What about jumping? Can you jump?
H: Yes, I love jumping.

- Then students can ask Hodori questions, using the given structures. Having a class mascot means that the teacher can present oral work with someone. Having another "speaker" around can make speaking situations easier to understand.

3) **Drawings**

- The teacher can use simple line drawings on the board.

4) **Silhouettes**

- The teacher can use silhouettes on the OHP. Silhouettes are useful when presenting verbs. Attach a small stick to them.

5) Puppets

- The teacher can use a paper bag with holes for eyes and mouth to create an animal, give it a name (e.g., Tony), and use it to help present new language. Also the teacher can use hand puppets made for language classrooms. When choosing these, make sure you can easily move the head and hands of the puppets with your fingers.

2. How to Practice Presented Language

1) Controlled practice

When new language is introduced to the students, it is important that the students try it out as soon as possible. In controlled practice, the activities are strictly controlled by the teacher, and students have little chance to express their own meaning. Repetition drills, dictation (see page 101 for examples), and ask-and-answer drills are examples of controlled practice. The focus is on grammar and structure rather than on communication.

T: What time is it?
Ss: It's ________

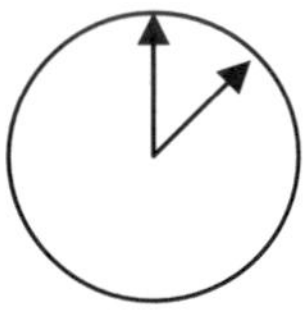

one o'clock

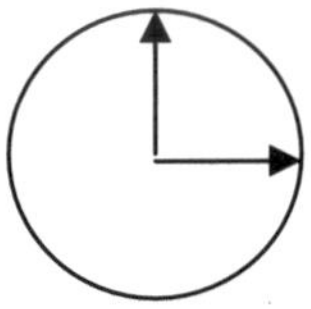

three o'clock

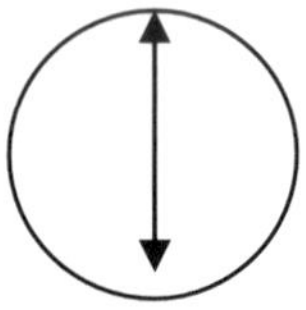

six o'clock

2) Guided practice

Guided practice follows controlled practice. These guided activities are done in pairs or in small groups. Guided practice gives students some choice (the answer is not predictable), but it is very limited. At this stage, students can change part of the given dialog.

A: What time is it? (They have a model clock.)
B: It's __________ (He puts the clock to the time he likes and answers.)

Speaking Activities

1. **Peer Tutoring**
   (1) The class is divided into several groups.
   (2) Group leaders come to the front.
   (3) Teacher teaches the group leaders first (e.g. What color is this? It's blue/green/black/red/yellow/white).
   (4) Each of the group leaders goes to his/her group and teaches.
   (5) Change group leaders for another teaching item.

2. **Jigsaw**
   (1) A story (or piece of work) is divided into 5 portions:

   One fine day, some mice played in the meadow.
   They were careful to watch for snakes.
   But the mice got sleepy, and forgot about snakes.
   They all took naps.
   While they slept, a hungry snake came looking for dinner.

   (2) The class is divided into 5 groups.
   (3) Each group is responsible for a specific portion of a story. They practice and memorize their story lines.
   (4) The class is re-divided into 5 groups.
   (5) Each group must learn the story by sharing information.

3. **Movement**

- Students get up from their chairs and go around the classroom to carry out an activity. Here is an example.

   (1) Students move around the room asking questions to discover fellow students who match some written descriptions. (Half of the students may move around to ask to avoid too much noise.)
   (2) They ask those students to write their names next to the appropriate description.
   (3) The student with the most names is the winner.

Find someone who

Has big eyes:
Has more than three brothers and sisters:
Has a birthday in January:
Likes chocolate ice cream:
Does not like cats:
Is wearing a watch:
Is wearing white socks:

4. **One-centered interview.** One-centered inverviews focus on one student. A student is interviewed by the rest of the class. Twenty questions is an example.

T: I'm a famous person. Who am I?
S1: Do you like dogs?
T: Yes.
S2: Do you live in Seoul?
T: Yes.
S3: Who lives with you?
T: My wife and two children.

5. **Roleplay**

- Students roleplay people in many different situations, e.g., going shopping, asking for help, visiting the doctor.

(1) Students listen to a model dialog of a roleplay.
(2) In groups they practice the dialog with role cards.
(3) In groups they roleplay the dialog assisted by role cards.
(4) Each group performs the roleplay in front of the whole class.

May I help you? It's 20 dollars. Here you are. You are welcome.

Yes, please. How much is that cap?. Okay. I'll take it. Thank you.

6. **The bottle game**

(1) All the students sit in a circle.

(2) The teacher gives the bottle "a spin" on the floor. When the bottle stops, the child who faces the top of the bottle asks a question to the child who is sitting opposite.

(3) If the child fails to answer or does not understand, then both of them are out.

(4) The teacher can prepare sentence cards (e.g., Stand up) for the game.

7. **Who will finish first**

(1) The class is divided into 3-4 equal groups. Each group has a face.

(2) The first child from Group1 throws the dice, and draws a part on his group face. (rules: 1-left eye, 2-right eye, 3-nose, 4-mouth, 5-left ear, 6-right ear)

(3) The first child from Group2 throws the dice, and draws a part on his group face.

(4) If a child gets the same number as another member of his group got earlier, he has to miss a turn. The next group throws the dice.

(5) The winner is the group who first finishes its face.

8. **Information gap activity**

(1) Each student has a copy of his/her schedule of activities for the week.

(2) In pairs, the students find an hour when they are free during the week to play tennis.

(3) They ask questions to find out when the other student is free.

A: Are you free at _____ on _______?
B: No, I have a piano lesson.
Are you free at _____ on _______?

Student A's schedule

	Monday	Tuesday	Wednesday	Thursday	Friday	Saturday	Sunday
4-5 p.m.	swimming lesson		homework	movies	piano lesson		soccer
5-7 p.m.	swimming lesson		homework	movies	piano lesson		soccer

Student B's schedule

	Monday	Tuesday	Wednesday	Thursday	Friday	Saturday	Sunday
4-5 p.m.		homework	bicycle	art lesson	piano lesson	swimming	soccer
5-7 p.m.			bicycle	art lesson	piano lesson	shopping	soccer

Task 1: Reflect

1. Think of the teaching methods in Chapter 2. Discuss how they are reflected in the speaking activities given in this chapter.
2. These are tips on teaching speaking. Add your tips to this list.
   (1) Conduct the class in English: The more English your learners hear and use in class, the better.
   (2) Use plenty of group and pair work: This maximizes the class time available for learners to speak.
   (3) Use guided activities where necessary: For learners with little experience in speaking practice, guided dialog can give confidence.
   (4) Link speaking to other tasks: In this way different types of speech can be practiced.

   (5) ______________________________
   (6) ______________________________
   (7) ______________________________
   (8) ______________________________

Task 2: Application

- Look at these speaking activities. Choose one and plan a lesson which focuses on speaking.

(1) Look and say

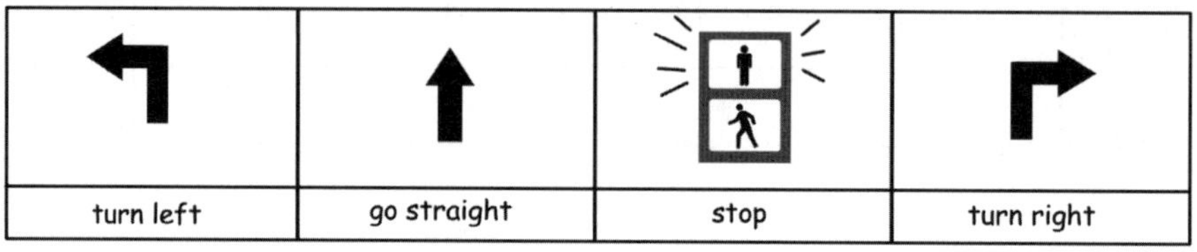

(2) Ask questions. Find the toy car.

A: Is it in the bag?
B: No, it isn't.
A: Is it on the table?
B: No, it isn't.

(3) Ask and answer

A: What do you do on Monday?
B: I go to art class.

Summary

In this chapter we have considered:

- ***Communicative competence***: This refers to the ability of native speakers to communicate effectively in their mother tongue. Communicative competence has four major skills (listening, speaking, reading, and writing) and four competences (grammatical competence, discourse competence, sociolinguistic competence, and strategic competence).
- ***The 3P teaching cycle***: A lesson focused on speaking has three steps: presentation, practice and production. Presentation and practice focus on accurate form and structure, while production focuses on meaning and communication.

- ***Speaking activities.*** There are many speaking activities emphasizing communication, such as peer tutoring, jigsaw, movement, one-centered, etc.

Useful Internet Sites

1. http://cybersight.com/cgi-bihn/cs/chat
2. http://www.globalvillage.com
3. http://www.englishclub.com

References and Additional Resources

Canale, M., and Swain, M. (1980). Theoretical bases of communicative approaches to second language teaching and testing. *Applied Linguistics, 1,* 1-47.

Nunan, D. (1999). *Second language teaching and learning.* Boston, MA: Heinle and Heinle.

Riggenbach, H., & Lazaraton, A. (1991). Promoting oral communication skills. In M. Celce-Murcia (Ed.), *Teaching English as a second or foreign language.* New York: Newbury House.

Scott, W., & Ytreberg, L. (1990). *Teaching English to children.* London: Longman.

Shrum, J., & Glisan, E. (1994). *Teacher's handbook.* Boston: Heinle and Heinle Publishers.

Chapter 9
Reading

Chapter Nine deals with the reading process, approaches to teaching reading to children, and reading materials and activities. It also presents tips for teaching reading. This chapter will give you the opportunity to build on your general ideas of reading instruction. In addition, the tasks included will strengthen your understanding of reading instruction.

In this chapter, we will consider:
(1) What is reading?
(2) What are the major theories on the process of reading?
(3) What are the main approaches to teaching reading to children?
(4) What types of materials and activities are useful for teaching reading?

What Is Reading?

◆ Read the passage and describe the clown.

The clown looks funny. He has a big mouth and small eyes. He is tall. He always smiles. He is happy when he sees people smile at him. He is an old man, but he is a happy clown.

- As seen in the above example, reading is a multi-level interactive process between the text and the reader. During the reading process, the text is analyzed at various levels, with units of analysis going from letters to words to sentences and then to the whole text. In addition, the reader uses his background knowledge in the process of understanding the text

(Spiro, 1968).

- Hence, reading, along with listening, is viewed as a receptive skill. But it is different from listening. In listening, the words are gone as soon as they are heard, but the written words can be reflected on and revised. Moreover, unlike speaking and listening, not every individual can learn to read. Educators spend time, money and effort teaching reading to children in elementary schools around the world. Children spend more time learning reading than any other skill. But some children, though they spend up to 12 years in school, do not become literate.
- Reading is central to the L2 learning process of children. Ghosn (1997) points out: "...carefully chosen children's literature allows children to develop their receptive language in entertaining, meaningful contexts and naturally invites them to repeat many of the predictable words and phrases, which children gradually take ownership of, and add to their receptive and productive language."

Theories on the Reading Process

- There are two opposing theories regarding what is involved in the reading process. One theory views reading as a "bottom-up" (or data-driven) process in which:

  (1) letters are transformed into phonemic representations, e.g., /sumi/ /laiks/ /kæts/;
  (2) phonemic representations are then transformed into word representations, e.g., Sumi – likes – cats;
  (3) words are assigned meaning;
  (4) words are combined into meaning-bearing sentences, e.g., Sumi likes cats;
  (5) meaningful associations are formed;
  (6) information is finally stored.

- The contrasting theory views reading as a "top-down" (or conceptually driven) process in which the reader:
  (1) has a text to read;
  (2) makes predictions as to what the text might be, based upon his/her prior knowledge;

(3) reads the text to confirm the predictions;
(4) constructs meaning;
(5) assimilates new knowledge.

- Rumelhart (1977) proposes an interactive model in which both data-driven information and conceptually driven information come together. In this model, reading is not viewed simply as a "bottom-up" or a "top-down" process. It is viewed as synthesizing both processes, integrating all knowledge sources.

Approaches to Teaching Reading to Children

- There are several different ways to introduce reading in English. No matter which approach teachers take in their reading lessons, they should remember that all approaches are ways to stimulate reading and are not an end in themselves. However, if children have a mother tongue which is not based on the Roman alphabet, teachers will probably find that they will have to spend quite some time teaching phonics and word recognition first (Scott & Yetreberg, 1990).

1. Phonics

- This approach is based on letters and sounds. Basically, teachers teach the pupils the letters of the alphabet, and the combination of letters, phonically – as they are actually pronounced – so that the letter h is pronounced /h/, c is pronounced /k/ or /s/, ph is pronounced /f/, s is pronounced /s/ or /z/ and so on.

- It is best to start off with three or four letters that can make up a word like "can," "cat," "can't." You can then show pupils how to pronounce /kæn/, /kæt/, and /kænt/.
- Although phonics can become very complicated as all the pronunciation rules are introduced, it can be a very useful way into reading for those learners who are not familiar with the Roman alphabet or who do not have a one-to-one relationship between letters and sounds in their own written language.

2. Word Recognition

- This approach is based on words and phrases, and generally uses a number of flashcards – words written on cards like this:

apple	boy	dog

- It is common to start by teaching everyday words which are already familiar to the children. Teachers show the children the word and say it while pointing to the object. The children repeat the word. This happens several times with each word.
- There are a lot of word recognition games which can be done at this stage such as matching words and pictures, pointing to the object on the card etc. This approach encourages children to recognize a wide range of words and phrases before reading a text.

3. Whole Sentence Reading

Moonbear loves books.

Big books.

- This approach is based on meaningful phrases and whole sentences often presented in the framework of a story which the children read for the first time. The words are not presented in isolation, but as phrases or sentences. Hence, flash cards (sentence cards) are often used in this approach.

4. Extensive Reading

- In extensive reading, children read large quantities of easy material in the language they are learning. They read for general, overall meaning and for information and enjoyment. Children select their own reading material, and are encouraged to stop reading if it is not interesting or if it is too hard.

- **Important points in extensive reading:**
  (1) The material should be easy to read;
  (2) The material should be interesting to the children;
  (3) Children should read for general understanding;
  (4) Children should ignore the words they don't know, and avoid using their dictionaries.

- **Why extensive reading:** Children improve their reading fluency and sight vocabulary (the words the eye can recognize quickly and accurately). They get pleasure from reading in English. They also have confidence because they can read in English.
- **What to read:** If possible, it's best to start up a simple self-access library in the classroom, including:
  - ♦ graded readers (books in which the language is controlled, with easier grammar and a limited vocabulary presented);
  - ♦ children's story books;
  - ♦ downloaded stories;
  - ♦ kids' magazines;
  - ♦ poems, etc.

5. Whole Language Approach

- This approach is based on the belief that language should not be separated into its component parts, but should be taught as a whole system of communication. This means that listening, reading, speaking, and writing are integrated into reading lessons.
- In this approach, students interact with the text and use language for their own purposes. They read a story, talk about it, write their versions of the story, and tell the story to their classmates.
- Typical class activities include:

(1) Reading aloud by the teacher.
(2) Question and answer activities.
(3) Journal writing.
(4) Writing stories (or making booklets) based on a text.
(5) Silent reading.

Task 1: Reflect

1. Some reading approaches were introduced in this chapter. However, the ongoing debate over the best way to teach children to read focuses on two methods: the phonics-based approach (a bottom up approach) and the whole language reading approach (a top down approach). There have been countless arguments for each side, but never an argument strong enough to convince people that either method is clearly better than the other. Talk about the pros and cons of both methods of teaching using the points presented below:

    - Pronunciation:
    - Vocabulary:
    - Accuracy:
    - Children's interest:
    - Creativity:
    - Understanding texts:

2. Talk about the method or approach you will be most likely to use when teaching reading to children

Reading Materials for Children

- There are several types of reading material for children. Reading lessons based on carefully selected passages may make reading more enjoyable and meaningful to the children.

1. Storybooks

- Storybooks include e-books as well as paper books. Reading storybooks is an ideal way for children to develop their reading skill. When children read storybooks, they encounter the same words and sentence patterns again and again, and they can learn them naturally.
- Children's first attempts at storybook reading should be picture-governed. Initially, children label the pictures and describe the actions presented in a storybook, but their comments are restricted to each page. At successive levels, children begin to build the story from page to page.
- At the final level, children's storybook reading becomes print-governed. Children move from imbalanced reading in which they may skip unknown words, sound out words excessively or leave nonsense words uncorrected, to being able to read independently.

2. Class Stories

- Instead of reading from books, teachers can make and use class stories as a starting point for reading. The advantage here is that teachers can photocopy the stories freely, making sure that everyone has a copy, and the children can color their own copies.

- For example, in a class where Snowman is used, the teacher may build up a short story about Snowman using a story-telling technique. When the teacher makes a book about Snowman, he can ask the children to help him with the illustrations.

3. Texts Based on the Children's Language

- The texts based on children's spoken language prove effective with beginner readers. The idea is that each student has his/her own written text which says what he/she wants to say. It is important that the teacher does not set the task beyond the student's ability to use English when working with this material.
- This type of reading material often includes a picture. It can be about something which has happened, or just about how the student is feeling. This example was written by a Cambodian boy.

This picture is in Cambodia. I have a small house and behind my house I have a blue mountain and the four mountains. Beside my house there's two coconut and one tree behind the house. Behind my house I have a small rice field. It just grows. In front of my house I have a small lake and in the lake it have some flower they call lily. In front of the rice field there's the path to walk. In the mountain there's many bird flying to another tree. There's clouds in the sky. (Adapted from Spangenberg-Urbschat & Pritchard, 1994, p.113).

4. Rhymes, Songs and Poems

- Poetry and music are universal in human cultures. Children love poems, rhymes and songs. These can be a motivating force in the language classroom.
- Poems, as seen below, can be an effective vehicle for highlighting the use of syntax and vocabulary. They also allow children to read an entire text and identify the main idea as can be seen in this example.

An Egg Is an Egg

An egg is an egg until it hatches.
And then it is a chick.
Branch is a branch until it breaks.

And then it is a stick.

Nothing stays the same.
Everything can change.

A seed is a seed until it is sown.
And then it is a flower.

A brick is a brick until there are many.
And then they become a tower.

Nothing stays the same.
Everything can change.

This baby was a baby until he grew.
And now he is a boy.
But you can always be a baby.
You will always be my baby.

Some things stay the same.
Some things never change.

- Rhymes and songs can be used to develop a feeling for the rhythm of oral and written English. Through them, children not only encounter the rhythm of English but also infer the meaning of the vocabulary and sentences in context. Rhymes and songs also help children gain fluency in reading.

5. Non-Prose Texts

- Non-prose texts, such as comic strips, maps and graphs, can be an important component of reading. For some children, this kind of reading may be new. Children need the ability to interpret non-prose texts. These are the major types of non-prose texts for children as suggested by Silberstein (1994):

Types	Characteristics
Comic strips	Comic strips can be used to practice recognizing relationships between ideas in texts and to practice students' critical reading skills.
Maps	Maps from the public transportation department, street maps, and road maps with mileage tables can be used to practice giving and receiving directions, and determining the most efficient route.
Graphs/ charts	Graphs and charts often accompany technical prose. Tasks can be developed that require children to work back and forth, discovering how information in the graphs and charts supplements and explains the prose.
Diagrams	Diagrams may accompany prose and provide important information and clues for comprehension. Children can be provided with practice in developing, completing, and comprehending diagrams.

Reading Activities

1. Phonemic Awareness and Phonics

- Phonemic awareness and phonics are not the same, but they are mutually dependent. Phonemic awareness focuses on the sound units (phonemes) which form spoken words. Phonics associates sounds to written symbols (i.e., the alphabet). Together, they help children develop word-recognition skills, namely the ability to sound out unknown words (Hults, 2003).
- Activities for phonemic awareness and phonics are:

  (1) Word Pairs: Say word pairs (e.g., bear, chair; fox, box; horse, hose), and ask children to identify the words that rhyme by touching their nose or making a funny face.
  (2) Word Search: Give children the word search table and make them find the words presented and read them.
  (3) Phonics Unscramble: Prepare a phonics unscramble worksheet.

(4) Make children solve the scrambled words, group and read them.

Word Search: "ar" words

R A C S G T O Y P T Q Z R R B
A E H G N K B T A R T U D L T
J Q M A P Y R H R R S J R T M
B L A R G E A A T Z N R C R Q
Q A A D A L A R M A R H L Z T
I H R E C F A D D W E D B X J
S A P N X T K P P H A N F W O

Search ART, BARN, CAR, HARD, LARGE, MARK, SHARP, YARD, ALARM, FARMER, GARDEN, JAR, HARM, START, YARN

Phonics Unscramble:
The words below need to be unscrambled and grouped.

sihp: ____________
sahep: ____________
oact: ____________
seehp: ____________
oesh : ____________
toab : ____________
hows: ____________
ophs : ____________

(5) Fill in the Blanks: Prepare several index cards with blanks (e.g., b _ _ t, sh _ _ , gr _ _). Show the children the first card, and tell them what sound the missing letters make (e.g., /ou/). Then, tell the children to write the complete word. Repeat the process with the remaining cards.

2. Labels

- Students label their desks, books, and bags with their names. The teacher labels furniture and objects in the classroom to make the students familiar with written English. There should not be too many labels, and they should be changed after a week or so. Children should be encouraged to look at the labels and talk about what is on them.

3. Posters

- Colorful posters that include a lot of written words can be of great interest to children. They gradually recognize more and more of the words on the posters. But we should present written words to children after they have encountered them orally. Often we can use advertising posters, or let children make posters.

4. Messages

- An English message board in the classroom may have simple messages from the teacher, like *Don't forget your crayons on Friday, No homework tomorrow.* It may have children's messages too: *My dog had 5 puppies, My birthday is on Saturday.*

5. Read and Look Up

(1) Divide the reading passage into word groups.
(2) Then the teacher reads the first word group,
(3) The students look up and speak it aloud from memory.
(4) This activity is efficient in improving short-term memory. It is also useful for intonation practice.

One day/ Minsu/ went swimming./ It was hot./ He called Kichol./ Kichol wasn't home./ So/ he went alone./

6. Dictionary Exercise

- Gradually, as students use the dictionary, the teacher needs to show them how to find the information they seek. In a dictionary there is a lot of information. Students can find information about pronunciation, spelling, syllable division, meaning, parts of speech, usage, and the derivation of a word. Moreover, most words have more than one meaning. Hence, a children' dictionary in which the core information of a word is listed is more useful. For dictionary exercises, the students may need to put the words in alphabetical order in advance. This is an example exercise.

☻ Look and put the words in ABC order.

7. Scanning

- Scanning is used to find particular information quickly in a text. For example, when you look for a telephone number or a name in an index, your eyes move quickly over the words until you find the particular information you are looking for. You ignore everything except the specific information you want. Scanning is directed and purposeful and extremely fast. These are scanning activities for children.

Activities	Characteristics
Find new words	Tell children to find synonyms or antonyms, giving them clue words that they already know.
Find a specified ad	Find an item, specified by the teacher, on a whole page of advertisements, or the time of a specific TV show on the entertainment page of a newspaper.

Compare details	Check a set of brochure cuttings to find e.g., which airlines offer midnight flights from Seoul to LA.
Shopping lists	List all the vegetables available on the different parts of a menu or find the cheapest soda in a brochure from a soda merchant.
Newspaper headlines	Cram a selection of newspaper headlines onto a worksheet and ask the children to find the one that treats a specific topic.

8. Skimming

- Skimming is used to quickly identify the main ideas of a text. When you read the newspaper, you're probably not reading it word-by-word, instead you're skimming. People often skim when they have lots of material to read in a limited amount of time. These are skimming activities.

Activities	Characteristics
Create a title	Compose an alternative title or subtitle for a text or for each paragraph of a text.
Decide the question	Decide what question the author sets out to answer.
Draw inferences	Draw inferences about the writer's attitude toward a situation or topic.
Select a title	Choose the most appropriate title for a passage from those listed on a separate worksheet or poster.
Compare values	Find the best value in a ____ (such as car, TV set, computer, or whatever you like) by looking at a set of similar advertisements.

9. Intensive Reading

- Intensive reading is reading in detail for a complete understanding of every part of a text. This involves the class in the close reading of a passage, normally a fairly short one.

Activities	Characteristics
Match nouns and verbs	Circle all the subject nouns or noun phrases and indicate the verb that goes with each one.
Split sentences	(1) Put a slash between the two or more parts of a longer sentence to show where it could be broken down into shorter sentences. (2) List the words that would be removed in the process.
Fill in the gaps	Read a gapped sentence or paragraph and provide suitable words for each gap.
Complete tables and charts	Complete a table or a chart to present some specified data visually.
Read and choose	Read a passage and choose from among multiple-choice items. These can be vocabulary, comprehension of detail or inference items.

10. Extensive Reading

- Extensive reading is reading for the pleasure of reading, not focusing on every single detail in a text. It implies a measure of freedom and noninterference from teachers. Even so, teachers have to show interest and allow the children to offer some form of feedback (Cross, 1995).

Activities	Characteristics
Wall chart	Put a poster on the wall, listing the books available. The children are allowed to initial the titles of the books they have read and award a mark out of ten to express their degree of enjoyment of the book.
Make summaries	Readers can be asked to write a short written summary of each storybook they read.
Keep records	Let children keep a little booklet, with the names of the authors, the titles and the dates on which they finished each book.

Tips on Reading Instruction

- **Develop an awareness of printed language and the writing system**: Children should be taught the basics about books--that they are read from left to right and top to bottom, that print may be accompanied by pictures or graphics, that the pages are numbered, and that the purpose of reading is to gain meaning from the text and to understand the ideas that words convey.
- **Teach the alphabet**: A strong predictor of the ease with which a child learns to read is his or her familiarity with the letters of the alphabet. This familiarity is a critical building block for learning to read. Engage the children in activities that will help them learn to recognize letters visually.
- **Teach children how to sound out words**: Model sounding out a word, blending the sounds together and saying the word. The ability to sound out new words allows children to identify and learn new words on their own. Give children stories containing words that reflect the letter-sound patterns that have been taught, and encourage them to sound out words whenever they are uncertain.
- **Help children develop fluent, reflective reading**: Help children learn to read fluently by requiring them to read new stories and reread old stories every day. Help children extend their experience with the words, language, and ideas in books by interactively reading harder texts with them and to them every day. Relate information in books to other events of interest to the children. Help students identify the main ideas presented in the text, as well as the supporting details.
- **Set aside time for independent reading**: All children need to understand that part of being literate is reading every day. A good plan is to set aside time every day apart from instruction -- 10 to 15 minutes during which children read books, magazines, or newspapers they choose themselves. When children finish reading, they need time to tell a partner what they've read. The idea is that they're using information they've picked up and are conveying it to someone else. That provides practice in thinking and comprehending.

Task 2: Practice and Plan

1. This is a sample reading lesson. Work in groups and demonstrate how to teach the lesson.

   (1) Introduce a dialog about buying things.
   (2) Students repeat the dialog aloud after the teacher.
   (3) Write the dialog on the board. Students read it line by line.
   (4) **Scrambled sentences.** Make sentence cards, and stick them on the board. Students read the sentences, and then put them in the right order. (They can unscramble the sentences in the form of a game.)

Yes. How much is this toy car?

May I help you?

OK. I'll take it.

It's 20 dollars.

   (5) **Scrambled words.** Students arrange the words of a sentence in the right order.

Example:

May
you

help

I
?

   (6) Make the text into a fill-in-the-gap exercise (just remove some key words). Students read the text and fill in the missing words.

May I _____ you?
Yes. How ______ is this toy car?
______ 20 dollars.
OK. I'll ______ it.

(7) **Paired dialog completion.** Students A and B have copies of the dialog in which different information has been left out. They complete their dialog by asking their partners questions.

Student A

____ I help you?
Yes. ____ much is this toy car?
______ 20 ______.
______. I'll ______ it.

Student B

May I _____ you?
_____. How ______ is this toy car?
It's _____ dollars.
______. I'll take it.

(8) **Dialog writing.** Students draw pictures with speech balloons and write the dialog.

2. Read the dialogue, and design a reading lesson.

Jinho: I'm from Korea. Where are you from, Chris?
Chris: I'm from Canada.
Jinho: Where are you from, Cindy?
Cindy: I'm from Australia.
Where is your room?
Jinho: It's on the first floor.

Summary

In this chapter, we have considered:

- ***What are reading and the reading process?*** Reading is the fundamental skill upon which all formal education depends. Since reading is central to the learning process, teachers should take some action to foster a positive attitude toward reading depending on the age and needs of the children. The reading process involves interactive activities that include discovery, planning, collaboration, and revision to create meaning.
- ***What are the main approaches to reading instruction?*** A reading approach is a way to start teaching beginning readers. There are several ways to teach reading in a foreign language. The five approaches were presented in this chapter: phonics, word recognition, whole sentence reading, extensive reading, and whole language.
- ***What materials and activities are useful for teaching reading?*** This chapter introduces lots of materials and activities for teaching reading. They can be a useful source for reading lessons.

Useful Internet Sites

1. Reading activities
   - http://www.abcteach.com
   - http://www.dltk-teach.com

2. Teaching reading
   - http://www.starfall.com

3. Storytelling
   - http://www.littlefox.co.kr
   - http://www.storyarts.org

References and Additional Resources

Cross, D. (1995). *A practical handbook of language teaching.* Hertfordshire: Phoenix ELT.

Spiro, R. J. (1968). Constructive processes in prose comprehension and recall. In R. J. Spiro, B. C. Bruce & W. F. Brewer (Eds.), *Theoretical issues in reading comprehension.* New Jersey: Lawrence Erlbaum Associates.

Ghosn, I. (1997). ESL with children's literature: The way whole language worked in one kindergarten class. *English Teaching Forum, 35*(3), 14-19.

Hults, A. (2003). *Reading first.* Creative Teaching Press.

Moon, C. & Raban, B. (1992). *A question of reading.* London: David Fulton Publishers.

Rumelhart, D. E. (1977). Toward an interactive model of reading, In S. Dornic (Ed.), *Attention and performance VI.* Hillsdale, New Jersey: Lawrence Erlbaum Associates.

Scott, W. A., & Ytreberg, L. H. (1990). *Teaching English to children.* New York: Longman.

Silberstein, S. (1994). *Techniques and resources in teaching reading.* New York: Oxford University Press.

Spangenberg-Urbschat, K., & Pritchard, R. (Eds.) (1994). *Kids come in all languages: Reading Instruction for ESL Students.* International Reading Association

Chapter 10
Writing

Chapter Ten explains the characteristics of writing and some issues related to writing and writing instruction. In addition, various methods of writing instruction and writing activities are presented. Through the tasks included in this chapter, you will have a chance to think about how to use your practical knowledge to teach writing to children.

In this chapter, we will consider:

(1) What is writing?
(2) How do teachers respond to children's writing?
(3) What are the major approaches to teaching writing?
(4) How are controlled writing activities different from guided writing activities?

What Is Writing?

(The cat swallowed the mouse and the mouse was fit. And then the cat went away.)

- As seen in this writing of the hungry cat, the meaning of a written piece can be complicated. At the most basic level, writing is a physical act of producing words and sentences using a pen or a computer. It is also a mental act of inventing ideas and organizing them into sentences and paragraphs (Sokolik, 2003). The child/author of the above story is good at both the physical and mental acts. As a reader, you probably could read the text and understand its meaning with little difficulty.
- As can be seen in this example, writing is also a natural process. It

involves the interplay between the writer, text and reader. Sometimes the relationship between these three elements is different in form and purpose. For example, a shopping list, a novel, a poem, and a diary are different in form and purpose.

- To take another example, the purpose of 'The Hungry Cat' might be to show what the child saw to the teacher and other children. The child's intended meaning is revealed both in the picture and the story. Following are some issues related to writing and writing instruction.

1. The Writing Process

- Current teaching of writing is shifting away from emphasis on the products of writing to the processes of writing (Norton, 2004). Scholars in writing processes ask what the act of writing involves, how skilled and unskilled writers act during the act of writing, how teachers can help students as they write. They have identified the processes involved in writing by observing writers.
- People usually talk about the writing process by dividing it into four elements. They are pre-writing, drafting, revising and editing.

  - **Pre-Writing**: Pre-writing means anything you do to prepare your ideas for writing. It includes brainstorming, outlining, making notes, making word stars and free writing. Some pre-writing activities are designed to make your ideas flow easily (brainstorming). Some are intended to show what you want to say clearly (outlining). Still others are designed to help you focus on a topic and organize it (word stars).
  - **Drafting**: Drafting is putting words, sentences and paragraphs on paper. It is what most people call "writing." There are two principles of drafting: (1) write as much as you can, (2) concentrate on what you want to say.
  - **Revising**: Revising means looking at what you have done and deciding whether it needs changing. During revising, you look at what is already on the page, change the content, or reorder the ideas. Revising is not, however, the same thing as editing. Editing deals with surface errors like spelling, subject-verb agreement, or punctuation.
  - **Editing**: Editing is fixing surface errors before publishing. By correcting errors during editing, you make your writing clearer for

your intended reader.

2. Correction

- When teachers read a piece of writing for correction, they focus on these two things:

    - ♦ The content: Are the ideas good? Are they put together in a way which is easy for the reader to follow?
    - ♦ The language: Children might invent an excellent story, but they might be unable to get it down in correct English. Hence it is essential for teachers to point out the language mistakes and help children write in correct English (Phillips, 1993).

- It may be difficult for teachers of large classes to correct the errors of all written work. That would be too time-consuming. But there are times when this needs to be done to give feedback, or to reassure children that their written work is taken seriously. Teachers' corrections are needed, too, when children are involved in free writing (Cross, 1995). Here are some techniques for correcting errors:

Spot check	Circulate when children are writing and tick the work that you look at. Underline errors for self-correction and give comments in the margin.
Peer marking	Have children mark each others' work whenever possible.
Pair work	Have some written tasks done as pair work. Get neighboring pairs to monitor and correct each others' work.

3. Responding

- Responding and evaluating are often parts of the same process, but the terms need to be distinguished. Evaluation often includes response and some response contains judgment, but not all response is evaluative or leading to a grade. Moreover, response to children's writing can come from various readers, including classmates, teachers and the writers themselves, whereas evaluation mainly comes from teachers and often has the form of comments to explain a judgment or a grade (Reid, 1993).

- Raimes (1983) suggests these basic principles about how to respond to children's writing.
  (1) Don't immediately reach for a pen or pencil and respond when you pick up a child's piece of writing.
  (2) Look for strengths as well as weaknesses, and first let the children know what the strengths are.
  (3) Have your own rules for handling errors. Explain the rules to the children before the writing activity.
  (4) Remember that when you respond to a child's writing, your main job is not to pass judgment, but to help the writer see what to do next.

- Here are some techniques teachers can use when responding to their children's writing.

Written comments	In order to write comments, you need to read the work through once before writing anything on it. Then note what the children have done well. After pointing out the strengths, let them know what to do to improve their writing.
Talks	Talks are one of the best ways to help children revise their work. Talking to children about what they have written is often the best way to find out what they were really trying to say.
Checklists	Checklists can be used by children as well as teachers. They can contain questions about spelling, grammar, content, and organization.
Peer review	Peer review gives children the opportunity to share their writing. If children are to learn writing as a means of communication, they should not only write regularly but also regularly get feedback from a variety of readers. Peer review groups work best in a large class.

Task 1: Reflect

1. How will you respond to this writing? Write your comments on each piece of writing as a teacher would.

   (1) Dear Borah
   Hi? Iam Hye-won. Thank you for come to my party. I like your present. Because I like Jungle book 2 movie. Is in it fun? What are you buy at my birthday place. Whan is your birthday. If you invite me I will come.
   Good bye

   (2) Dear Hyewon
   Hi! I'm Borah!
   I think you are spider! Ha Ha just kidding! Did you have funtime at your birthday pirty? Did you have fun with your friends? I am so having a fun at you birthday pirty! We to play we having fun, we see the movie toghther I love it! What aboun you? You like it? You didn't like it, is in it boring to you? Heh? Any way I think you are like it!
   Bye bye!

2. Look at the above writing again and devise a checklist that children can use to check their writing.

Approaches to Teaching Writing

- Teaching writing to children has a number of advantages. Scott and Ytreberg (1994), and Raimes (1983) point to these advantages of writing instruction:

  (1) It diversifies learning activities by adding hands to eyes and ears.
  (2) It lets children express their personality and opinions. It helps children become more involved with the new language.
  (3) It helps to strengthen learning in other skill areas. Writing activities help memorization, speaking and reading practice.
  (4) It helps to develop a conscious awareness. When children write, they have the time to go back and think about what they have written. Hence writing lessons can reinforce the grammatical structures, idioms, and vocabulary that children have been learning.
  (5) Writing is valuable in itself. Students can feel satisfied and confident when they see their work in print.

- All things considered, what might be the best method of writing instruction? Perhaps no one can answer this question. There are so many answers since there are so many different teachers, teaching styles, learners and learning styles. However, here are some common approaches you can use when you teach writing to your students.

1. The Controlled Writing Approach

- This approach is sequential. Children are first given sentences, then paragraphs to copy or to practice. For instance, they are given sentences and asked to change questions to statements, present tense to past tense, or singular nouns to plural nouns. They can also practice a particular grammatical item. This approach emphasizes accuracy rather than fluency or originality. Here is an example activity.

◆ Write these words in the paragraph below the picture (adapted from Holt, 1997, *High Five 5*, p.32).

(flew, were, played, went, was, saw, ate, left, took)

Yesterday, we __________ to the river. We ________ our kites. Then, we __________ with a ball in the river. We ______ hungry, but Tom and Jim ________ the food on the train. Then Jim ________ a mango tree. We ________ the mangoes. It ______ a great day.

2. The Free Writing Approach

- This approach teaches writing by assigning vast amounts of free writing with only minimal correction of error. This approach emphasizes content and fluency, not language and grammar. For instance, a student writes about what he learned and the teacher comments on it. The audience (reader) is viewed as another important element in this approach. Here is an example (Mannix, 1994).

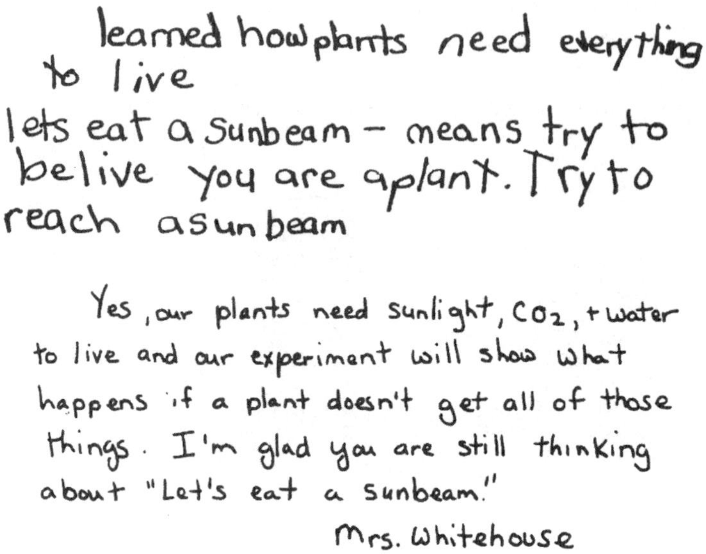
learned how plants need everything to live
lets eat a Sunbeam - means try to belive you are a plant. Try to reach a sunbeam

Yes, our plants need sunlight, CO_2, + water to live and our experiment will show what happens if a plant doesn't get all of those things. I'm glad you are still thinking about "Let's eat a sunbeam."
Mrs. Whitehouse

(Learned how plants need everything to live. Let's eat a sunbeam – means try to believe you are a plant. Try to reach a sunbeam.

Yes, our plants need sunlight, CO2 + water to live and our experiment will show what happens if a plant doesn't all of those things. I'm glad you are still thinking about "Let's eat a sunbeam." Mrs. Whitehouse)

3. The Paragraph Writing Approach

- This approach stresses organization. Children copy a paragraph, analyze its organization and imitate this in a writing exercise. This approach is based on the principle that people in different cultures organize their writing in different ways. In a classroom using this approach, the children can

  (1) put scrambled sentences into paragraph order,
  (2) identify general and specific information,
  (3) choose or invent an appropriate topic sentence,
  (4) insert or delete sentences.

4. The Communicative Approach

- This approach stresses the purpose of a piece of writing and a specific audience for it. Child writers are encouraged to behave like writers in real life. They set up the purpose of their writing with a specific audience in mind. Teachers may extend the readership to other children in the class. The readers read the piece of writing, respond, or give comments. The teachers may specify readers outside the classroom, and thus provide child writers with a broader context from which to select appropriate content, language, and style.

5. The Process Approach

- This teaching method concentrates on the process of writing. Children are encouraged to think about a topic, to share drafts with teachers and peers, and to use each draft as a beginning for the next. They do not write in a restricted time and hand in their writing for the teacher to correct. Teachers give their children crucial support: enough time and good feedback. In a classroom using this approach, the writing instruction becomes a process of discovery for the children. They discover new ideas and the language to express these ideas.

Task 2: Reflect

- What do you think is the best method of teaching writing? Why?

Writing Activities

- Writing activities go from being tightly controlled to being completely free. Teachers in ESL/EFL situations will usually do more controlled or guided activities with beginners, but they should not exclude very simple free activities. In general, controlled and guided activities are being done to practice the language. Concentration is on the language itself. Free writing activities allow for self-expression for low level writers. Here, content is what matters most (Doff, 1988). Table 1 compares three types of writing activities.

Table 1. Comparison of Three Types of Writing

	Controlled Writing	Guided Writing	Free Writing
Focus	Language	Language and meaning	Meaning
Errors/mistakes	Controlled	Partly controlled	Not controlled
Chance to express one's ideas	Not allowed	Allowed in a limited way	Allowed

- As shown in the above table, both controlled and guided writing activities practice the language, such as grammar, vocabulary and structure. In controlled writing activities, the teacher controls the activities completely. The children have little chance to express their ideas. In guided writing activities, the children can express their ideas in a limited way. Those writing activities are very structured, and students practice communicating using structured models. In free writing activities, on the other hand, meaning is more important than grammar. Here, the students write freely for communication.

1. Controlled Writing Activities

(1) Straight copying

- Copying words and sentences helps children see the connection between the written and the spoken language. For children who find even straight copying difficult, you may let them trace words and sentences. Here is an example (Eisele and others, *Hip Hip Hooray! 2*, p.32).

(2) Copying with correction

- Children rewrite a given sentence or a paragraph. They change incorrect details. The sentences can be nonsensical to give fun to the writing exercise like:

> ◆ Correct the underlined words and write the sentences again.
>
> A beautiful girl is singing merrily in the train. <u>His</u> dad and mom are listening and smiling. All the passengers in the <u>bus</u> feel happy.

(3) Matching

- Children copy the sentence or word which matches a given picture. Or they choose what they want to write about the picture and copy it.

Write one sentence: ________________________________.

A. She is cooking.
B. She is studying.
C. She is washing clothes.
D. She is cleaning her room.

(4) **Organizing and copying**

- Copying can also be used to practice structured writing, as in the example below:

> 447 Song-Hyun Dong, Dal-Seo Gu,
> Daegu City
>
> November 10th, 2004
>
> Dear dad,
>
> Hello, Dad. How are you?
> Daegu is really fantastic. ………………………………………………
> …………………………………………………………………………………
> Yesterday …………………………………………………………………
> …………………………………………………………………………………
> Tomorrow …………………………………………………………………
> …………………………………………………………………………………
> I will see you soon.
>
> Love,
> Il-Ok

It has big, beautiful mountains.

I am going to visit Daegu Museum.

I went to Duryu Park.

I enjoyed roller-skating there.

There are a lot of parks.

(5) Cloze passages

- Teachers select an easy passage, remove a few words from it, and make photocopies. In cloze passage writing, teachers may focus on a specific area of vocabulary or grammar. The average rate of deletion in a paragraph will be every 5th or 6th word. One or two words in a sentence can be deleted. Here is an example.

◆ Fill in the blanks with the following words: Lee, me, we, my, good, came.

In my English class, _____ wrote a story. Miss _____ gave me a very _____ grade. When my dad _____ home, I showed him _____ English story. He told ____ it was very good.

2. Guided Writing Activities

(1) Picture sets

- A picture sequence, such as a comic strip, provides the subject matter for writing a narrative and for speculating about the story beyond the pictures in the strip. It also provides material that offers guidance on vocabulary and sentence structure. Children write a list of sentences about a picture sequence frame by frame.

9:00 am	2:00 pm	7:00 pm

(2) Fill-in exercises

- These are useful for beginning learners. Since most of the language is given, students are not required to produce much language. Here is an example.

  My Pets
  We have 3 family pets: a dog, a cat and a tortoise. The dog's name is Ben. The cat's name is Nero. The tortoise's name is Toto.

  My Pets
  We have ______ family pets: ________________________________.
  ____.
  ____.
  ____.

(3) Dictation

- The teacher dictates only half a sentence, and asks the students to complete it in their own way. Here is an example.

  I like ____________________________.
  I love ____________________________.
  I don't like ________________________.
  I hate ____________________________.

(4) Picture description

- The picture taken from a magazine or a poster can be used for description. This could be a famous person, a domestic scene, an event, or a well-known place. A good way to begin is by having the children write a few questions about the picture. These questions can then be answered in the form of a written description. You may provide vocabulary needed.

(5) Letters, cards, invitations

- Writing letters and cards seems to be a popular class activity. It is indeed a useful way of getting children to write short meaningful pieces of writing. A child writes a letter and sends it to one of his classmates, who then answers the letter. Here is an example.

To __________,

Are you free on ____________________?

I am going to have a ____________________ party.

Will you come to ____________________________?

You can ___________________________________.

Maybe it will be fun. Call me if you can ____________.

The number is ________________________________.

Love,

Jinho

3. Free Writing Activities

(1) Letters, e-mails

- Letters and e-mails are two of the most widespread forms of written communication. Letter writing gives children the chance to deal with a variety of forms and functions that are an essential part of language learning. We write letters or e-mails to invite, explain, apologize, congratulate, complain, and thank. Each of these language functions has its own associated vocabulary, sentence structure and organization.
- Teachers can present a situation to the class, such as inviting friends to a birthday party. They then show the class a sample letter of invitation and explain the form and mechanics. The children then write invitations to their birthday party.

(2) Daily notes

- Many people keep daily notebooks or journals. They write a record of the events of the day and their ideas about those events. This personal writing can be used in the classroom. For this activity, teachers ask children to keep a special notebook and to write in it in English for a few minutes every day. These daily notes can be the students' reaction to something they saw or read, or a description of their feelings or about an event.

(3) Story completion

- Writing group stories is a good idea since the actual writing can be shared. Teachers should make sure that children do lots of pre-writing activities so that they have the ideas and the words they need for story writing. Children need to understand that most pieces of writing are written to be read by others. So the final version should be on a large piece of paper which can be posted on the wall of the classroom.

(4) Diaries

- At the beginning of each week, and before a weekend or holiday, children describe their own plans and activities. While they are writing, teachers circulate, check their writing and give information. Later each child reads his/her weekend plan aloud to the whole class.

Other Writing Activities

1. Picture dictionary
   (1) Give students a topic which is easy to draw (car).
   (2) In their exercise book, they draw the object and name the parts (door, tire, window, driver).
   (3) Students circulate and look at others' drawings. They ask the names of the parts which they do not know.
   (4) As the students learn the new words, they add them to their drawing.

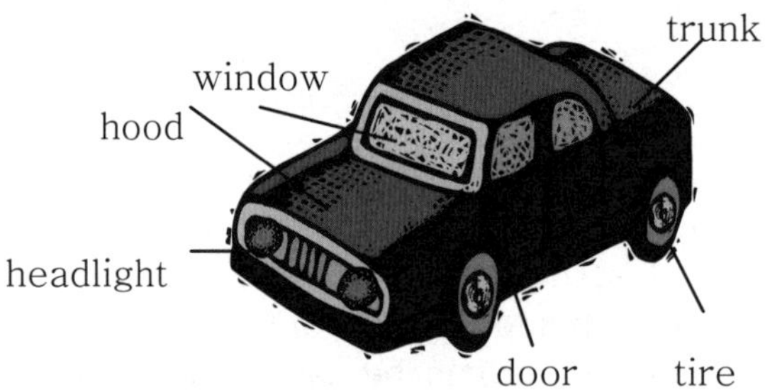

2. The merry alphabet

(1) In pairs or groups, students write some English letters in a column:

A
B
C
D

(2) They write one word with the first word beginning with the letter A, the second with the letter B, the third with the letter C and so on, for example: Apple

Bag
Cat
Door

(3) Then each pair or group comes to the front, and writes words with another set of letters, e.g., E, F, G, H.

(4) The pair who finishes writing words first wins.

3. Five favorite words

(1) Students select their five favorite words and write them down on a piece of paper.

(2) The students form pairs.

(3) In pairs they negotiate and write a new list of five words on a piece of paper.

(4) The teacher collects the lists and redistributes them so that each pair of students has a different list.

(5) The pairs write sentences using the words on the list.

(6) The pair who completes writing first wins.

4. Tennis

(1) Students work in pairs with one sheet of paper between them.

(2) They toss a coin to see who starts.

(3) The first person "serves" by writing a sentence which is true.

Examples are:

We speak Korean.
We are tall.
We like kimchi.

(4) The second person can accept the "serve' and return it by writing a second sentence. He/She can call a fault. A fault occurs when the information is not correct (We don't speak Korean.) or the sentence is

not grammatically correct (We likes kimchi.).

(5) The game continues, scoring as for tennis, until one wins.

5. The rainbow game

(1) Students write four colors they like on their worksheets.
(2) The teacher dictates 15 nouns, and the students write each word in one of the appropriate columns.
(3) As each student reads a list aloud, his classmates guess which color is intended.

blue	white	green	red

6. Choose your words

(1) Prepare the following grid and make one copy for each group of 4 students.
(2) Divide the class into groups of four.
(3) Distribute the grid and blank sheets of paper.
(4) Each group orders the words and writes this on the paper.
(5) Students then add words to complete the sentence.
(6) The group who uses all the words on the grid and makes the most sentences wins the game.

blue	ten	books
picture	red	green
one	pen	bag

7. Swat!

(1) Students work in groups.
(2) Each group writes words about a certain topic (food).
(3) One student comes to the front, and writes the words on the board.
(4) Two students come to the front, and hold flyswatters.

(5) The teacher or group leader gives a command to swat one of the words (Swat the juice.).

Summary

In this chapter, we have considered:

- ***What is writing?*** Writing is both a physical act (typing words and sentences using a computer) and a mental act (inventing a story). It is also an interactive process between the writer, text and reader. The relationships between these three elements may be different in form and purpose.
- ***What are the issues related to writing instruction?*** There are some key elements teachers should know in order to teach writing well: the writing process, correcting, and responding. The writing process includes the four steps: pre-writing, writing, revising and editing. How to correct and respond is important for teachers who wish to help children add depth to their writing and improve their general writing skills.
- ***The three types of writing activities*** Writing activities in this chapter are presented according to the level of control the teacher assumes over the activity. In general, controlled and guided activities are for practicing the language itself, and free activities are carried out to express ideas.

Useful Internet Sites

1. Web sites for children
   - http://www.write4kids.com
   - http://kids.ot.com
   - http://a4esl.org

2. Web sites for teachers
   - http://yn.la.ca.us/cec/ceclang/ceclang-elem.html
   - http://www.efl4u.com

References and Additional Resources

Cross, D. (1995). *A practical handbook of language teaching.* Hertfordshire: Phoenix ELT.

Doff, A. (1988). *Teaching English to children.* New York: Cambridge University Press.

Eisele, B., Eisele, C., Hanlon, R., Hanlon, S., and Hojel, B. (2004). *Hip hip hooray!* London: Longman.

Holt, R. (1997). *High five.* Edinburgh: Longman.

Manix, K. (1994). Let's eat a sunbeam. In N. Hall & A. Robinson (Eds.*), Keeping in tough* (87-99). London: Hodder & Stoughton.

Massi, M. P. (2001). Interactive writing in the EFL class: A repertoire of tasks. *The Internet TESL Journal, Vol. VII,* No. 6, http://teslj.org/

Norton, D. E. (2004). The effective teaching of language arts. New Jersey: Prentice Hall.

Nunan, D. (1998). *Language teaching methodology.* Hertfordshire: Phoenix ELT.

Phillips, S. (1993). *Young learners.* Oxford: Oxford University Press.

Raimes, A. (1983). *Techniques in teaching writing.* New York: Oxford University Press.

Reid, J. M. (1993). *Teaching ESL writing.* New Jersey: Prentice Hall Regents.

Scott, W., & Yetreberg, L. (1994). *Teaching English to children.* London: Longman.

Sokolik, M. (2003). Writing. In D. Nunan (Ed.), *Practical language teaching* (87-108). Boston: McGraw Hill.

Chapter 11
Grammar

Chapter Eleven examines the relationship between L1 acquisition and grammar, defines grammar, and deals with how to teach grammar. It also introduces the guided participatory method proposed by Shrum and Glisan, along with their four-stage lesson plan for teaching grammar. The activities provided in this chapter include a number of grammar-focused games that can be used in the classroom. Through the tasks included in this chapter, you will have the opportunity to apply theory to teach grammar in the classroom.

In this chapter, we will consider:

(1) What is grammar?
(2) What are the main grammar teaching methods?
(3) What is the four-stage grammar instruction method suggested by Shrum & Glisan?

Acquisition of Grammar by L1 Children

- Grammar plays a key role in communication for young children. According to Moon (2000), by about four and a half years of age (before school age), L1 children acquire the basic grammar system needed for everyday communication.
- Children learn grammar indirectly and unconsciously. It is often said that they pick up the language on the streets and at home. Grammar here includes pronunciation, spelling, vocabulary, and sentence formation.
- Cameron (2001) also states that by the age of 5, acquisition of basic grammar by children is complete. They acquire more complex aspects of grammar in their teens, and continue to extend their vocabulary afterwards. This is because some aspects of grammar and vocabulary are connected to written language which they learn later. In the following table are some examples adapted from Perera (1989).

Table 1. Acquisition Age of Grammatical Structures

Structures	Age of acquisition
• relative clauses (whose),	11
• preposition + relative pronoun (in which)	11
• co-ordinators (but, yet)	11
• linking words (although, unless)	15

- As seen here, children often do not use some structures until they are in their early teens. This is because these structures occur in written texts which children generally encounter in their early teens. Some linking words (unless, whether, however, etc.) occur in children's speech around age 15. These linking words are difficult for young children to learn because, in order to use the linking words correctly, they need to develop a logical understanding of their meaning in a sentence.

What Is Grammar?

- You may ask yourself the questions "What is grammar?" and "What is its role in communication?" Let's examine the following passage from the writing of a nine-year old Korean child:

today is shopping day
I am went waterfront
saw many book, costume, toy
I did not buy any thing
because wig is not
(Today was a shopping day. I went to the waterfront. I saw many books, costumes and toys. I did not buy anything, because I didn't see the wig I wanted.)

- In the above passage, the child seems to be more concerned with expressing meaning rather than form. She lists content words (today, shopping, waterfront, saw), but does not use function words (for, to, I, the) often. She is good at expressing meaning, but not good at producing correct sentences.

- As seen in the above example, the grammar of a language is the way to connect words and to produce correct sentences. In other words, grammar includes the method of combining sounds/words together into sentences/discourses. Consider this diagram (Cameron, 2001; Ur, 1988):

  Phonology/Vocabulary → (Grammar) → Sentence/Discourse

- Hence, grammar is a very essential part of a language. Nobody can be free from the use of grammar when they speak a language. Even though their knowledge of grammar is incomplete, they should connect words and make sentences in their speech or writing. Without this their language would be chaotic. Hence we should combine the words in a correct and accurate way when we express ourselves.
- As they develop their grammatical ability, children start to produce discourses (which needs more advanced grammar) and make their utterances socially appropriate in the context. Once the grammatical system of the language is acquired, children are able to process a great number of utterances. In this regard, learning a new language means acquiring the grammatical system of the language.
- A learner who knows the grammar of a language is one who has mastered these rules and can apply them to express himself/herself. For example, "*This is a book*" is grammatically correct, while "*This are a book*" is not. To know grammar in this case means understanding the rule: a singular subject (*a book*) is combined with a singular verb (*is*).

◆ **Grammar**: The grammar of a language includes various rules of pronunciation, spelling, vocabulary, and sentence formation. Simply speaking, it enables the speaker to combine words and produce sentences.

How to Teach Grammar

- Grammar is essential for successful acquisition of a language. Without grammar, our speech or writing would be only a list of unconnected, meaningless words and phrases. How can we teach grammar to children?

Do we have to teach directly (deductively) or indirectly (inductively)?

1. Deductive Method

- Many scholars agree on the benefits of grammar teaching, but very few agree on how to teach grammar. Higgs and Clifford (1982) advocate an explicit method of grammar teaching. According to Higgs and Clifford, the teacher should explain grammar explicitly and give special exercises to learners so that they can learn grammar rules efficiently. One problem with the method of explicit grammar teaching is that most of the exercises the teacher gives the learners are based on artificial contexts, so the drills based on the following dialogue would be meaningless to them:

  T: What is your name? (T already knows his name.)
  S: I am Minsu.

- Another problem with the method of direct grammar teaching is that it gives the learners a passive role in learning grammar. In the classroom where this teaching method is used, learners would listen to plenty of their teacher's explanations about grammatical rules, but they would have very few interactive activities between themselves. A knowledge of grammar rules does not necessarily lead to communicative competence. This is why many scholars doubt the value of direct grammar instruction.

2. Inductive Method

- The scholars who advocate implicit grammar teaching methods (Krashen, 1985; Terrel, 1977; Dulay and Burt, 1973) don't agree with the idea that we should teach grammar to the learners directly. For example, Krashen (1985) suggests that students can acquire grammar naturally if the teacher provides them with sufficient comprehensible input. For him, this follows the way children acquire their first language in natural settings.
- The indirect teaching method is sometimes called the inductive teaching method, since the child has to induce grammar rules from comprehensible input. A problem with the method of inductive grammar teaching is that it can be a waste of time if the learners are not motivated to learn their target language and do not discover grammar rules correctly. Furthermore, we cannot guarantee that learners will hypothesize, test, and re-

hypothesize a set of grammar rules on their own.

- When the EFL learning situation is taken into account, it becomes more obvious that the method of indirect grammar instruction has serious shortcomings. Ur (1988) states that learning EFL is different from L1 acquisition. In natural learning (such as the learning of children's first language), the amount of time and motivation devoted to learning is so great that teaching grammar is not essential even though it is typical for teachers to consciously plan grammar instruction. Sooner or later, the learners will acquire their first language including grammar. However, in an EEL classroom as described in Chapter 2, there is much less time available, and often less motivation, which indicates that learning time has to be organized for optimum efficiency.

3. Participatory Method

- Some scholars prefer an alternative method in teaching grammar. Shrum and Glisan (1994) suggest a compromise between the explicit and implicit methods. They call their method a guided participatory method, and propose a four-stage grammar instruction: presentation, attention, co-construction of the grammar explanation, and an extension activity. Table 2 illustrates the main features of each teaching method.

Table 2. Grammar Teaching Methods

Inductive method	Participatory method	Deductive method
Learners analyze grammar explanation for themselves.	Teachers and learners collaborate on grammar explanation.	Teachers provide grammar explanation for learners.

- **Presentation:** The teacher presents an interesting story, poem, TPR, etc., which includes the grammatical structure in question. During this stage, the meaning of the text is the main focus. Let's look at the poem below. The teacher introduces this writing and reads it aloud to the students several times. He/She can use a set of pictures, TPR, role-play, or sounds to help the students understand the meaning of each phrase.

By Myself
When I am by myself
And I close my eyes
I am a twin
I am a dimple in a chin
I am a room full of toys
I am a squeaky noise
I am a gospel song
I am a gong
I am a leaf turning red
I am a loaf of brown bread
I am whatever I want to be
An anything I care to be
And when I open my eyes
What I care to be
Is me

- **Attention**: Once the learners understand the overall meaning of the poem, the teacher turns their attention to focus on grammar, i.e., some aspects of the language used during the presentation stage. The teacher can ask some questions about sentence patterns, and words and phrases repeated in the text. For example, the teacher can ask these questions:

T: What sentence pattern is used the most often?
S: "I am a ______."
T: How many "I am a ___" sentences are there?
S: Nine.
T: Can you write down all the "I am a ___" sentences on your notebook?

- **Co-construction of the grammar explanation**: Both teacher and learners co-construct the grammar explanation. The teacher has her learners focus their attention on the target form and helps them understand it. During this step, it is very important for learners to guess what the target form is. For example, the teacher may ask the questions:

T: What words come after "I am a"?
S: twin, dimple in a chin, room full of toys…
T: What kind of words are they?
S: Person words, thing words, food words…

T: Can you say another sentence using "I am a ______"?
S: I am a small fish in the sea.

- **Extension activity**: The learners use the grammatical structures and carry out a task. The extension activity provides them with the opportunity to use their new skill in a creative way. It includes information-gap activities, role-plays, games, and writing projects. For example, the learners may write a poem using the structure, "I am a ________." They may be allowed to use the same opening and closing lines in their poem like this:

When I am by myself
And I close my eyes
I am a ________
I am a ________
I am a ________
I am a ________
I am a ________
I am a ________
I am a ________
I am a ________
I am whatever I want to be
An anything I care to be
And when I open my eyes
What I care to be
Is me

Task 1: Reflect

- Let's suppose you teach "Yes/No questions" to your students. Plan a lesson, focusing on the grammatical structure, "Are you a ________?," "Yes/No, I _______". Here is an example.

A: Are you a cow?
B: No, I'm not.
A: Are you a deer?
B: No, I'm not.
A: What are you?
B: I'm a goat.

Some Tips on Grammar Instruction

- **Don't expect too much**: Remember that children learn ESL/EFL grammar slowly. Some children learn English at an early age, but they tend to make slow progress, and overall gains are not directly linked to the time spent. It is not desirable to expect rapid grammatical improvement from young learners (Wharton & Race, 1999).
- **Expect errors**: Children make errors when they learn a language. By making errors, they experiment with the language and develop a set of rules. That means that children do not simply imitate words and sentences, but they work out how the language system operates and build up their own language system by making errors. Errors are evidence that learning is taking place.

- **Use discovery techniques**: Many textbooks recommend that the teacher use a combination of discovery and presentation techniques. These two techniques are of great importance in teaching children grammar. To do this, the teacher needs to show learners examples of a grammatical item in various contexts and encourage them to work out its significance. This activity shows an example:

Look at the pictures. Ask and answer with your friends.

A: What did she/he/they find?	B: She/He/They found a bat/ball/bag.
A: Where was it?	B: It was under a tree.

find → found do, does → did

- **Capitalize on learners' existing knowledge**: Before you teach children grammar, try to find out what knowledge they already have. Even if the rules they know are incomplete, you may find them useful in teaching the grammar in the new lesson.

Grammar Activities

1. **Finding twins (adjectives)**
   (1) Materials: a grid showing adjective-noun combinations (Box 1).
   (2) Procedure:
   ① Each student is given an adjective-noun table (Box 1), and he/she practices the words/phrases needed for the activity.
   ② Each student chooses one word in each column.

   e.g., *big black cat*
   fat white mouse

   ③ The students move around and each student finds someone else with the same choices by asking, "Do you have ____?" questions:
   e.g., *Do you have a big white cat?*
   Do you have a small brown dog?
   ④ The students who find the most twins win the game.

Box1. I have a …

big	black	dog
small	white	cat
fat	brown	mouse

2. **Guessing game (adjectives)**
   (1) Materials: a set of 9 to 12 cards. One adjective-noun phrase is written on each card (Box 2).
   (2) Procedure:
   ① Students have the set of word cards (Box 2) and practice them before they play the game.
   ② Cards are placed in a pile face down on the desk.
   ③ They play in groups. Each student, in turn, takes a card, and tells

the others only what the noun is.

④ The others guess the entire phrase.

S1: Table
Ss: A round table?
S1: No.
Ss: A wooden table?
S1: Yes.

④ The student who correctly guesses the phrase gets the card. At the end, the one who has the most cards wins the game.

Box 2. A tall man

A tall man	A fat baby	A brown cow
A happy girl	A red light	A long story
A big bed	A wooden table	A boring book

(Cut into individual cards)

3. Miming (adverbs)

(1) Students practice the words (Box 3) before they play the game.

(2) One student (i.e., the person who guesses) leaves the room or closes his or her eyes.

(3) The teacher selects an adverb of manner (e.g., slowly), and shows it to the class.

(4) The student outside the room comes in and gives a command to the group (e.g., Stand up. Sit down. Turn around. Smile.) If the adverb chosen is "slowly," then the students are supposed to do their actions slowly. From their actions, the guesser guesses the adverb.

(5) If the student who guesses cannot identify the adverb, he or she needs to give another command.

S1: Stand up.
Ss: (Stand up slowly.)
S1: Fast.
Ss: No.
S1: Sit down.
Ss: (Sit down slowly.)
S1: Slowly.
Ss: Yes, that's right.

Box 3. Slowly

Slowly	Happily	Sadly	Lovingly	Fast

(Cut into individual cards)

4. **Frequency surveys (adverbs)**
   (1) Materials: questionnaire sheets (Box 4).
   (2) Procedure:
      ① Students are given the questionnaire (Box 4), and practice the sentences first.
      ② Students work in pairs, asking each other questions using Box 4:
         S1: How often do you watch TV on Sunday?
         S2: Often. How about you?
         S1: Sometimes.
      ② Students report their results to the class, using full sentences:
         Tom often watches TV on Sunday. He never watches TV on Monday. He often plays computer games on Saturday. He sometimes plays computer games on Tuesday.

Box 4. How often do you…?

How often do you … often – sometimes – never
1. …watch TV on Sunday?
2. …watch TV on Monday?
3. …play computer games on Saturday?
4. …play computer games on Tuesday?
5. …read comic books on Friday?
6. …read comic books on Wednesday?

5. **Erasing pictures (negative sentences)**

(1) The teacher draws a picture on the board.
(2) Students say what has to be erased, using negative sentences:
   A: Tony doesn't have a ball.
   B: Tony doesn't have a cap.
(3) The teacher erases the ball and then the cap. This goes on until the board is empty.

6. **Comparing pictures (negative sentences)**
   (1) Materials: one set of pictures (for each pair of students, A and B) (Box 5)
   (2) Procedure:
      ① Students work in pairs, each having one of the paired lists.
      ② Each student describes an item to the other student.
      ③ The objective is to find out if they describe the same item or not.
      ④ If they describe the same item, the two students make a circle around the picture. If they describe the two different items, they make an X on the picture.
      A: Number 1 is a boy.
      B: Yes, it is a boy.
      A: He is walking.
      B: No, he is making a plane.
        (They x the item.)

Box 5. Number 1 is...

7. **Don't say no (negative sentences)**
   (1) The teacher makes a list of questions (Box 6) on the board.
   (2) One volunteer comes to the front.
   (3) The class asks him or her questions from the list.
   (4) The volunteer must give true answers. He must not say "no." If he says "no," another student comes to the front and answers the questions.
   (5) All the answers must be in full sentences.

A: Are you Jinho?
B: I am not Jinho.
A: Are you American?
B: I am not American.

Box 6. Are you…?

Are you Jinho/Youngsu/American/Chinese/Japanese?
Are you old/cold/hot/hungry/thirsty/tall/short/strong/weak?

8. **Telephoning (numbers)**
   (1) The objective is to find out the phone numbers of the students.
   (2) Each student has a sheet of paper (or a list of names with blank spaces for phone numbers) and writes down his/her phone number.
   (3) One student tells his or her number and calls up someone else.
   A: This is 523-3412, Jinho speaking. Are you there, Minsu?
   B: Yes, this is Minsu. My number is 567-2345. Are you there, Insuk?….
   (4) As the game goes on, each student writes down the phone numbers of the people he/she speaks with.

Box 7. My phone number is …

Name	Phone number

9. **Detectives (possessives)**
   (1) Let one student leave the room, or let her close her eyes. This student is a "detective."
   (2) Pick up one object that belongs to any student and show it to the class.
   (3) The detective comes back in and asks one of the students,
   A: Is this yours?
   B: No, it isn't mine. It's his. (indicating the direction where the true owner is sitting)
   (4) Students may lie until the true owner is found.
   (5) The detective moves around the class, and finds the owner of the object.

10. Whose is it? (possessive pronouns)

(1) Materials: small objects like pencil cases, mirrors, sunglasses, and hairpins, bags, caps, etc., which belong to the students.

(2) Procedure:

① The teacher moves around the room and collects some small objects belonging to the students.

② She places the objects on a table.

③ She makes sure the students know the words (e.g., pencil case, mirror, sunglasses, hair pin).

④ Each student makes a grid (Box 8), and writes the names of as many owners of the items as he can remember.

⑤ Check students' answers using possessive pronouns:

T: Is this yours, Mira?
A: No, it isn't mine. It's Kicheol's.
T: Is this yours, Kecheol?
B: Yes, it's mine.
T: Okay. This pencil case is Kicheol's.

⑤ The winner is the one who has the most correct answers.

Box 9. Is this yours?

Pencil case	
Mirror	
Sunglasses	
Bag	
Hair pin	
Eraser	

11. Memory game

(1) Materials: 1 set of small cards for each group of 4 to 6 students. Each card depicts a person or animal doing some simple action (Box 6).

(2) Procedure:

① Students look at the cards and say the sentences several times.

② Students work in groups of 4-6.

③ Each group has a set of cards spread out face down.

④ The first participant turns over any two cards, and describes them:

He is swimming.
She is skating.

⑤ Then he or she replaces them face down.
⑥ This is repeated until all the cards are turned over and replaced.
⑦ Now the memory game starts, beginning with the first participant.
⑧ The aim is to remember where the cards are located. The player first describes the card and then turns it over. If the sentence is correct, he keeps the card. If not, he replaces it.
⑨ Each card becomes the property of the student who voices the correct sentence and turns the card up.
⑩ The winner is the one who has the most cards.

Box 6. He/She is swimming (*Elementary School English 5*).

12. What do I do (simple present)

(1) Materials: copies of forms showing various themes or activities (sports, food, hobbies, clothes, subjects, animals, countries) (Box 7).

(2) Procedure:

① Ask students to write one thing they do in each of these areas.
Sports: I watch tennis.
Food: I eat pizza.
Hobbies: I collect stamps.
② Then the students get into pairs and talk about their activities.
③ Each student tells the class about his or her partner:

Yunhi watches tennis. She eats pizza. She collects stamps…

Box 7. Things I do

Sports	
Food	
Hobbies	
Subjects	

Task 2: Application

1. Miss Lee, an English teacher, decides to try discovery techniques in her grammar teaching. She previews the lesson, and sees that she will need to teach negative sentences. She picks a context for the new structure, the morning routine. For her presentation, she writes the following sentences on the board:

I get up early in the morning.	I don't get up early on Sunday morning.
I wash my face and hands.	I don't wash face and hands on Sunday morning.
I have breakfast.	I don't have breakfast on Sunday morning.
I brush my teeth	I don't brush my teeth on Sunday morning.

Miss Lee reads the sentences aloud. The students seem bored, uninterested. She then asks a question: "What do you see here?" The students are bewildered and silent. Miss Lee calls on Minsu. He says, "sentence beginning with I ." Miss Lee thinks to herself, "These students are not ready to discover grammar rules." She stops asking questions and explains the rules of negative sentences directly.

(1) How would you evaluate Miss Lee's grammar lesson?
(2) What type of presentation would you choose to teach negative

sentences?

(3) How would you plan the lesson if you were Ms Lee?

2. Let's look at the following lesson plan, which focuses on describing persons and things (adjectives). Answer these questions briefly.
   (1) What method do you think the teacher is using in teaching 'adjectives'? (If necessary, reread the three grammar teaching methods in this chapter.)
   (2) Why do you think the teacher teaches this way?

The Lesson "He Is Strong."

Objectives:

To describe things and people.
To sing a song describing people.
To tell a story describing people.

(1) Look and Say (Presentation): Using pictures and objects, the teacher introduces new vocabulary and sentences. (long, short, tall, big, small, strong, weak, beautiful, handsome; It/She/He is ______. I am ______.). Students understand the meaning of the words/sentences and practice them by repeating them after the teacher.

(2) Listen and Find (Listening): The teacher describes the pictures introduced in Activity (1), and the students listen and choose the right pictures.

(3) Whispering game (Speaking): The teacher divides the students into four groups. They sit in four lines. The first student in each group whispers a sentence using a picture card from Activity (2). Each student whispers to the one behind until the last student stands and speaks the sentence.

(4) Sing Along: The students sing this song with motions.

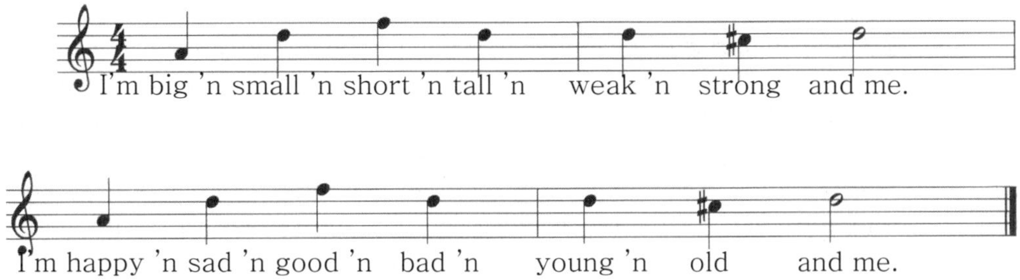

(5) Retell the Story

- Students have a set of picture cards (7 cards) which together tell a story. Each picture card depicts the meaning of a sentence in the story.
- Before they start the game, they practice the sentences first with the help of the teacher.
- The teacher and the students sit in a circle.
- The teacher looks at each picture card, tells the sentence and passes the picture to the student sitting next to her who will then repeat the sentence and pass the card to the next student who does the same.
- This continues around the circle and with each card; sometimes simultaneously.
- (The Story) His name is Taemin. He has a mother and a father. He has a sister and a brother. Taemin is tall. His brother is short. His sister is thin. Taemin has a happy family.

Summary

In this chapter, we have considered:

- ***What is grammar?*** Grammar is a very essential part of a language. It is a tool by which a speaker combines sounds and words and produces a variety of sentences. As they develop their grammatical ability, children start to produce sentences and discourse and make their utterances correct and socially appropriate to the context. Once acquired, grammar enables children to produce a great number of utterances. In this regard, learning a new language means acquiring the grammatical system of the language.

- ***L1 acquisition and grammar.*** Grammar plays a key role in communication for young children. English L1 children acquire the basic grammar system needed for everyday communication by learning it indirectly and unconsciously. It is often said that they pick up the language on the streets and at home. Grammar here includes pronunciation, spelling, vocabulary, and sentence formation. It is known that by the age of 5, the acquisition of basic grammar by children is generally complete. They acquire more complex aspects of grammar in their teens, and continue to extend their vocabulary afterwards.
- ***How to teach grammar.*** There are two main grammar instruction methods, deductive and inductive. In the deductive method, the teacher explains grammar explicitly and gives special exercises to the learners. The problems with this method are that the exercises are based on artificial contexts and that the learners learn grammar passively. In the inductive method, students learn grammar indirectly from the language given to them. They are believed to work out grammar rules from the material. The problem with this method is that the learners can waste their time if they do not discover grammar rules correctly. Shrum and Glisan (1994) suggested a guided participatory method and proposed a four-stage grammar instruction: Presentation, Attention, Co-construction of the Grammar Explanation, and an Extension Activity.

Useful Internet Sites

1. Grammar from the British Council
    - http://www.learnenglish.org.uk
2. Grammar from English Center
    - http://ec.hku.hk/vec/grammar/default.htm
3. Interactive grammar exercises
    - http://www.stufun.com
4. Teaching grammar
    - http://www.eslpartyland.com

References and Additional Resources

Cameron, L. (2001). *Teaching languages to young learners*. Cambridge: Cambridge University Press.

Moon, J. (2000). *Children learning English*. Oxford: Macmillian Heinemann English Language Teaching.

Dulay, H., & Burt, M. (1977). Should we teach children syntax? *Language Learning 23*, 245-258.

Higgs, T. V., & Clifford, R. T. (1982). The push toward communication. In T. V. Higgs (Ed.), *Curriculum, competence, and the foreign language teacher*. Lincolnwood, IL: National Textbooks.

Krashen, S. (1985). *The input hypothesis*. New York: Longman.

Perera, (1989). *Children's writing and reading: Analyzing classroom language*. Malden, MA: Blackwell Publishers.

Shrum, J., & Glisan, E. (1994). *Teacher's handbook: Contextualized language instruction*. Boston: Heinle and Heinle Publishers.

Terrel, T. (1977). A natural approach to second language acquisition and learning. *Modern Language Journal 61*, 325-337.

Ur, P. (1988). *Grammar practice activities: A practice guide for teachers*. Cambridge: Cambridge University Press.

Wharton, S., & Race, P. (1999). *500 tips on TESOL*. London: Logan Page.

Chapter 12
Lesson Planning

Chapter Twelve presents the format of a lesson. It focuses on introducing the basic structure of a lesson and its major components. Attention is given to presenting the organization and use of teaching materials. The tasks given in this chapter will present real teaching situations, offering you the chance to use your understanding to plan a lesson on your own.

In this chapter we will consider:
(1) What are the main components of Cameron's lesson plan?
(2) What are the main components of the traditional five-step lesson plan?
(3) What are the content elements you must consider when you plan a lesson?

Planning a Task

- There is no standard lesson plan. Teachers write their lesson plans on the basis of their teaching experience and teaching situation. Of course, novice teachers will need some guidelines about how to plan and carry out a 40-minute lesson. This chapter introduces the basic organization of a lesson and its major components. Before we look at an example lesson plan, let's consider how to plan a simple task.

1. The Three-Step Plan

- It is common to plan a task in three steps: pre-task, task, and post-task. This three-step format can be applied to reading as pre-reading, reading, and post-reading. It can also be applied to other skill tasks (e.g., prelistening, listening, and post-listening). Cameron (2002) suggests this teaching format:

(1) Preparation
- Warm up
- Presentation

(2) Core Activity
- Practice
- Production

(3) Follow up

- Preparation activities prepare the learner to carry out the core activity successfully. The main function of these activities is to make the core activity less demanding for the learner. Introducing and practicing new language items is a good example. The core activity is the main body of teaching. It includes the practice of the items presented and the use of them for communication. The follow-up activities build on successful completion of the core activity. A lesson may have a number of follow-up activities. Writing activities after an oral work can be used as a follow-up.

2. The Key Features of a Task Plan

- In planning a task, we should keep in mind these key features:

(1) The task has meaning and purpose for students. A good classroom task has a clear meaning and purpose for the students. Through carrying out the task, the students should satisfy certain interests, like knowing about the hobbies of their friends.

(2) The task has clear teaching goals. A classroom task should have language teaching goals for the teacher. The goals should be clear enough so that at the end of the task, the teacher is able to tell whether his goals have been accomplished or not.

(3) The task has a beginning and end. A task should have a clear beginning and end. It may be short or it may last over several lessons. However, both teacher and students should be able to sense when a task begins and ends.

(4) The task actively involves the learners. A task may involve the learners in pairs or in groups. However, being exposed to English

through the task is not enough. A desire to communicate in English and active participation are crucial if language development is to occur.

A Task: Ann's Weekend

- Let us see how the three-step format is applied to a task in the classroom. Let's suppose we have a textbook which presents the following task. How will you plan the task?

	morning	afternoon	evening
Saturday	(1) watch TV	(2) take a nap	(3) play outside
Sunday	(4) go to the bookstore	(5) play video games	(6) practice the piano

- **Ann's weekend:** This is Ann's weekend plan. Look at the table and say sentences with your partner *(Let's Go 3*, p.25).

An Example Lesson Plan

1. Preparation
   (1) The teacher introduces the action verbs, and the names of the objects and places, using pictures.
   (2) The students practice the words and expressions in groups and pairs.
   (3) The teacher introduces the action verbs in past form. To help the

students to understand why past verbs are needed, the teacher makes the weekend a particular one that has already passed.

watch → watched
take → took
play → played
go → went
practice → practiced

(4) The students practice the past verbs in pairs.

2. Core Activity

(1) The teacher introduces model sentences using the grid.

Saturday morning, Ann watched TV.
Saturday afternoon, she took a nap.
Saturday evening, she played outside…

(2) T-S practice: The teacher points to a box and students say the sentence.
(3) S-Ss practice: S1 comes to the front, points to a box, and the rest of the students say the sentence.
(4) Pair practice: S1 points to a box, and S2 says the sentence.
(5) Group practice: The students make a group of four, and make up appropriate sentences about their last weekend.

3. Follow Up

(1) The teacher writes key words on the board next to the pictures.
(2) The teacher writes sentences from the grid.

Saturday morning, Ann watched TV.
Saturday afternoon, she went swimming.
Saturday evening, she watched TV….

(3) The students write more sentences and complete the writing about Ann.
(4) The students write some sentences about their last weekend.

Task 1: Practice

- Plan each of the tasks. Make sure your plan includes the three major steps, preparation, co-activity and follow-up.

1. **Let's Make**: Let's make a paper dog. Follow the instructions.

1. 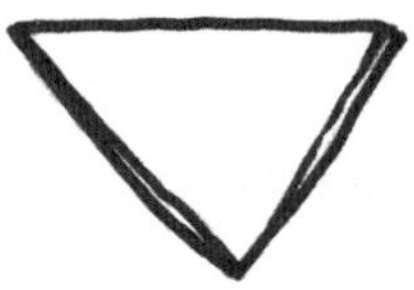 Fold the paper and make a triangle.	4.  Fold this corner and make a triangle. This is a nose.
2. 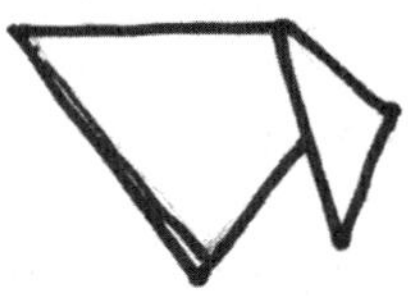 Fold this corner and make a triangle. This is an ear.	5.  Draw two circles. These are eyes.
3. 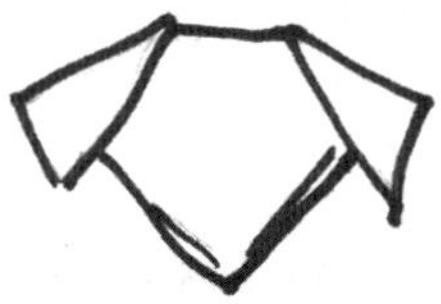 Fold this corner and make a triangle. This is an ear, too.	6.  What is it? It's a dog.

2. Let's Talk

A: When is your birthday? B: It's April 1st.

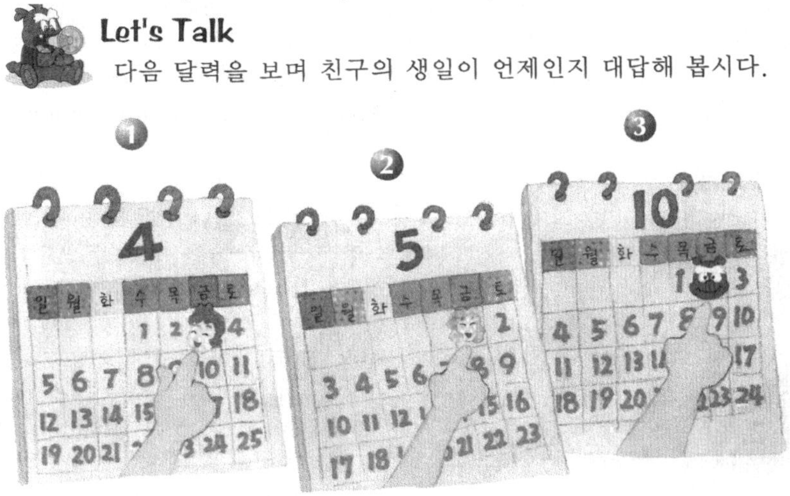

3. Let's Play

A: How much is this? B: It's 200 won.
A: Okay. I'll take it.   B: Here you are. Thank you.

A Lesson Plan

- Here is an example of a detailed lesson plan. The first part of the plan contains information about *what* the teacher is going to teach (content). The second part describes *how* the teacher is going to teach (procedures). The following is the story for the lesson adapted from Cameron (2001).

- The Story

Once upon a time, there was a little fish. He lived in a big river with many other fish. But he was not happy. All the other fish were very beautiful. Their bodies were of many different colors, red, blue, yellow, purple, and so on. His body was white. He felt very sad. "I want to have a beautiful body like those other fish," he said.

So one day he went to see the king of the river. He was a big, black eel who lived in a big black hole at the bottom of the river. He swam down and down and down to the bottom.

"Who is there?" said a loud voice.

"It's me, little fish," said the little fish.
"What do you want?" said the eel.
"I want to have a beautiful body, please." said the little fish.
"What color do you want?" asked the eel.
"Please make my body red," said the little fish.
And his body became red.
"Please make my tail yellow," said the little fish.
And his tail became yellow.
"Please make my fins green," said the little fish.
And his fins became green.
"Please make my face orange," said the little fish.
And his face became orange.
"And make my lips red," said the little fish.
"You rude little fish. You did not say please," said the big black eel.
"I won't give you any more colors."
So the little fish had white lips. But he was very happy, because his body

had many colors. He was very beautiful.

1. Lesson Plan Part 1: Content (what to teach)

- **Background information** Age: 10 Time: 40 mins No. in class: 38

- **Objectives (What you want students to achieve by the end of the lesson.)**
  (1) Follow a set of instructions and color the fish accordingly.
  (2) Tell others in class about the colors of the fish.
  (3) Give an opinion about the little fish.
  (4) Enjoy the story.

- **Language skills (listening, speaking, reading and writing.)**
  (1) Listen for details.
  (2) Follow spoken instructions.

- **Function (The reasons why the sentences are used, e.g. to describe, to greet, to buy things.)**
  (1) Describe the colors of the fish, e.g. His body is red. His tail is yellow.

- **Vocabulary (The known and new words students will use in the lesson)**
  (1) New vocabulary: parts of fish (body, tail, fins, lips), eel, adjectives (angry, sad, rude, beautiful, many colored).
  (2) Known vocabulary: face, colors (red, yellow, blue, orange)
- **Language structure (The language patterns that students will use)**
  (1) Instructions: e.g. Make my body red.
  (2) Use of *'please'* to make instructions polite.
  (3) Use of past tense: e.g., Once upon a time there lived a little fish. He lived.
- **Teaching aids (The visual and audio aids to support the lesson)**
  (1) Pictures of fish, eel, word cards
  (2) Colored paper, blank sheets of paper

2. Lesson Plan Part 2: Procedures (how to teach)

Steps	Teacher's Activity	Students' Activity
Preparation	**1. Warm-up** Brief review of colors, using a team game.	Students stand in lines behind flags of different colors. As the teacher says a color, the students behind the flag of that color sit down.
	2. Introducing the topic. Bring in a picture of a gold fish. Discuss the fish, e.g. what it looks like, its color, and parts. Check who has fish at home. Practice key words.	Students tell what they know about fish. They tell about their own fish. They practice new key words.
	3. Introducing the story. Tell the students you are going to tell a story. Get them to guess what will be in the story.	Students guess what will be in the story.
	4. Explaining the activity. The students color their fish as they listen to the story. Give out crayons and blank sheets for the fish drawing.	Group leaders give out crayons and blank sheets of paper.
Core activity	**5. Core Activity**. Tell the first part of the story with actions and pictures. Continue the story. Make sure the students color their fish as they listen.	The students color their fish following the teacher's instructions.
Follow up	**6. Follow up 1.** Get the students to compare drawings.	The students compare to see if they have the same.
	7. Follow up 2. Go around the class, and the students describe the colors of their fish, e.g. His body is red.	Some students say the colors of their fish.
	8. Follow up 3. Ask students what they thought about the story, the eel, and the little fish, e.g. The eel is a good fish…	Students give their opinions.
	9. Follow up 4. Display the students' colored fish on the wall.	Students write their names and help the teacher to display the drawings.

The Five-Step Lesson Plan

1. The Key Components

- This traditional five-step lesson plan is well known.
  (1) Warm up: Teacher greets the class, reviews the last lesson, makes small talk
  (2) Presentation (Introduction): Teacher introduces new topic, language, and pronunciation.
  (3) Practice (Model the language): Students practice the new language in the form of drills.
  (4) Production (Application): Students use the new language in communication games.
  (5) Round up: Teacher reviews the key expressions, and gives homework. Teacher may use the same pictures and cards used during the presentation and practice stages.

2. Types of Interaction

- For interaction or practice, the whole class is divided into pairs, or groups. In general, after the new language is introduced through a whole class activity, the students practice the language in pairs and/or groups.

  (1) Whole class activity: There are two types of whole class interaction, teacher-students (T-Ss), and student-students (S1-Ss). In T-Ss interactions, the teacher speaks to the whole class, and in S1-Ss interactions, one student plays the teacher.
  (2) Pair work: Students practice language and interact with their partners. The advantage of pair work is that all the students are involved in the learning activities at the same time, and that the teacher can move around the class to check their practice.
  (3) Group work: Students work in groups of 4 or 5. Group work is useful when practicing dialogs in which three or more people speak.

3. A Sample Lesson Plan

<table>
<tr><td>Date: 11/10/04</td><td colspan="2">Grade: 6th</td><td>Teacher: Carol Ann Moyer</td></tr>
<tr><td>Objectives</td><td colspan="3">• Ask others what they did yesterday.
• Tell others what you did yesterday.</td></tr>
<tr><td>Steps</td><td colspan="3">Procedure</td></tr>
<tr><td>Greeting</td><td colspan="3">T: Good afternoon class.
Ss: Good afternoon.
T: How are you today?
Ss: Fine, and you?
T: I feel great. Are you happy today?
Ss: Yes.
T: I'm glad to hear that.</td></tr>
<tr><td>Presentation</td><td colspan="3">T: Are you ready to listen? Two people are talking.
Listen carefully. (p.275 Teacher's Guide)
T: Let's practice some of Suyoung and Youngjae's dialog.
(Guided practice in groups and with partners using this handout.
____ What did you do yesterday?
____ I went to the Science Museum.
____ The Science Museum? Wow!
____ What did you do yesterday?
____ I played basketball with my cousin.
____ That sounds fun.</td></tr>
<tr><td>Practice</td><td colspan="3">T: You spoke loudly. That's great!
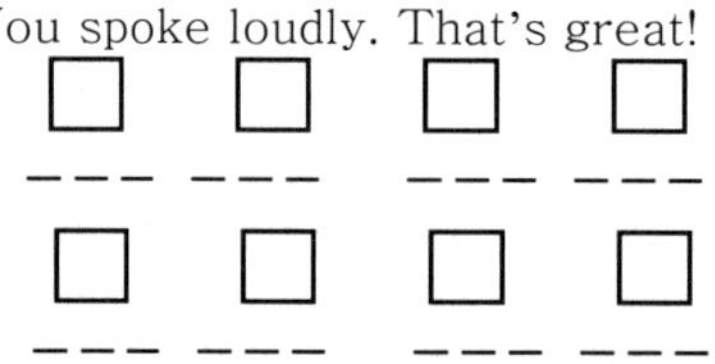
(8 pictures with sentence strips. E.g., I went swimming.)
T: Look at this. (Teacher points to the picture of a swimmer.)
This is my picture. Can you ask me a question?
Ss: What did you do yesterday?
T: I went swimming. (The teacher places the correct sentence strip under "her" picture.)
T: Let's read the other 7 activity cards/sentence strips.
(Teacher reads, students repeat.)
(The teacher chooses a student to be "teacher".)
T: Can you ask this "teacher" a question?
Ss: What did you do yesterday?</td></tr>
</table>

<table>
<tr><th>Steps</th><th>Procedure</th></tr>
<tr><td rowspan="3">Production 1
(Guessing Game)</td><td>S1: Points to an activity card and reads. E.g., I watched TV. Then she/he puts the card below the correct picture.
(Repeat 6 times with new "teacher".)</td></tr>
<tr><td>(Places 2 sets of pictures face down on the board with activity cards off the side but readable.)
T: Let's play a game. This side of the room is the red team. This side of the room is the blue team.
T: What did you do yesterday? Did you go to the doctor? (while pointing at the activity cards.) One student will answer the question e.g., No, I played soccer, and if he/she finds the correct picture, that team will get 1 point. The teams will take turns guessing which picture is which activity.
T: You did well. The ____ team won today. Good job.</td></tr>
<tr style="display:none"><td></td></tr>
<tr><td>Production 2
(Survey)</td><td>T: Now I want to know... "What did YOU do yesterday?"
Look at this paper. Write your name here. (T shows the place.)
I'll read the questions and you write yes or no below your name.
<table>
<tr><th>Did you....?</th><th>Students' name</th><th>Carol teacher</th></tr>
<tr><td>play the piano</td><td></td><td></td></tr>
<tr><td>play a video game</td><td></td><td></td></tr>
<tr><td>play soccer</td><td></td><td></td></tr>
<tr><td>play basketball</td><td></td><td></td></tr>
<tr><td>go to the zoo</td><td></td><td></td></tr>
<tr><td>go swimming</td><td></td><td></td></tr>
<tr><td>go shopping</td><td></td><td></td></tr>
<tr><td>watch TV</td><td></td><td></td></tr>
</table>
T: Now, please ask me about yesterday.
Ss: "What did you do yesterday?" "Did you play the piano?" ...
T: (Respond with a start and answer each question.)
For example, "Did you play the piano?" "No, I didn't. I can't play the piano." "Did you go shopping?" "Yes, I did. I got new shoes.
T: Now write another student's name in the next column. It's marked with an X. Ask each other the "Did you ..." question. Write their answers below their name. Do not show your worksheets to each other.</td></tr>
<tr><td>Closing</td><td>T: Time is up. You did a good job today. Thank you.
Ss: Thank you.</td></tr>
</table>

Task 2: Application

1. Revise the lesson plan on the little fish to create a five-step format.

2. Read this story and plan a lesson. Use the five-step plan (or the three-step plan). You can change the story somewhat in order to emphasize your teaching goals.

Curious George

Once upon a time, there was a little monkey. His name was George. George lived in Africa. He was a good little monkey. He had a long tail, small ears, long arms, and short legs. He had a long, thin body. He had big eyes.
He was always very curious.
One day George saw a man.
He had on a large yellow hat.
The man saw George too.
"What a nice little monkey," he thought.
"I 'd like to take him home with me."
He put his hat on the ground.
George was curious.
He came down from the tree.
He looked at the large yellow hat.
He picked it up and put it on.
The hat covered George's head.
He couldn't see.

The man picked George up and put him into a bag. The man went home with him.

References and Additional Resources

Cameron, L. (2001). *Teaching languages to young learners.* Cambridge: Cambridge University Press.

Celce-Murcia, M. (Ed.) (1991). *Teaching English as a second or foreign language.* New York: Newbury House.

Frazier, K., & Nakata, R. (1994). *Let's go 3.* Oxford: Oxford University Press.

Rivers, W. M. (1981). *Teaching foreign language skills.* Chicago: University of Chicago Press.

Scarcella, R., & Oxford, R. (1992). *The tapestry of language learning.* Florence: Heinle & Heinle Publishers.

Shrum, J. L., & Glisan, E. W. (1994). *Teacher's handbook.* Boston: Heinle and Heinle Publishers.

Chapter 13
Classroom English

Chapter Thirteen concerns teaching English in English. It focuses on answering the question, "Why should you use classroom English?" and examines the advantages and disadvantages of using English in the English classroom. Then, some handbooks about classroom English are introduced. This chapter also considers the questions, "Where and how can you learn classroom English expressions?" and "How can you teach classroom English to students?" Further, this chapter will offer you the opportunity to practice classroom English in pairs or groups.

In this chapter, we will consider:
(1) What is classroom English?
(2) Why should you use classroom English?
(3) Where and how can you learn classroom English expressions?
(4) How can you teach classroom English to your students?

Why Should You Use Classroom English?

- An ESL/EFL teacher has to talk a lot in the classroom. She tells students what to do. She gives language input for learning. She controls the class. She gives feedback to students. It is primarily through her verbal instruction that teaching and learning take place. Classroom English is the English which the teacher uses in order to teach her students in the English classroom.
- Willis (1981, p. xiii) states that teachers should teach English through English as often as possible (for example, when introducing new words, showing how to play a game, chatting with the students, etc.).

- Why should you use classroom English as much as possible in your classes? Gardner and Gardner (2000) point out that when you teach English in English both you and your pupils would get the following benefits:

(1) Learners recognize that the English lesson is quite different from other lessons such as social studies, history, math, etc.
(2) Learners develop thinking skills in English.
(3) Learners learn actively.
(4) Learners gain confidence in replying to your instructions or questions.
(5) You create a good English-speaking atmosphere.
(6) You increase your own confidence in using English as an EFL teacher.

- Similarly, Moon (2000, p. 63) provides a list of the advantages and disadvantages of using English to teach English, as shown in Table 1.

Table 1. Advantages and Disadvantages of Using English to Teach English

Advantages	Disadvantages
Students are exposed to more language input.	When a teacher uses English, it can take a long time to explain things.
Students gain confidence when replying to the teacher's instructions or questions.	Slower learners may be frightened or put off by having to use English.
Teaching in English provides real reasons for using English to communicate.	A teacher may have limited English, and therefore he/she may be a poor role model.
Students pick up much classroom language without their teacher's direct instruction.	Students may not express what they have learned in English because of their limited English.
Students are motivated to learn English actively.	Slower learners may not be motivated to learn English with enthusiasm.
Using English will help students develop thinking skills in English	Due to teaching in English it may take longer to cover the syllabus.

- Moon goes on to provide these guidelines on using classroom English with young children:

(1) Language:
  - Use simple commands (Look here) or questions which require single word responses (What's this?).
  - Use short sentences (They match).
  - Use repetitive patterns (What's this? What's that? What's in the box?)
  - Use simple, familiar vocabulary.

(2) Actions:
  - Link the words to the actions.
  - Use objects and pictures.
  - Involve children by letting them help the teacher.

♦ **Classroom English**: the English the teacher uses in the classroom to teach her students.

- These examples show how to speak classroom English with actions.

(1) Sit down, please.

(2) Stand up, please.

(3) Quiet, please.

(4) Watch and listen.

(5) Say it louder, please.

(6) Say it quietly, please.

(7) Say the whole sentence.

Task 1: Reflect

- Work in groups. Discuss how much you agree or disagree with these viewpoints.

  (1) For low-level students, instructions should be given in English and then their L1.
  (2) Teachers should try several other ways to get their meaning across before using their L1.
  (3) Teachers should always use English in the classroom, because their L1 may interrupt students' progress toward proficiency in English.
  (4) Using translation to give the meaning of new words or structures helps students think that English and their L1 have a direct correspondence.
  (5) Giving instructions in English is essential, because it is an opportunity for genuine communication in English in the classroom.
  (6) Getting a learner to translate instructions or explanations or sentences for the class helps everyone understand them correctly.
  (7) Students should always use English in the classroom.
  (8) Students should have the opportunity to discuss, in their L1, the differences and similarities between the language which they are learning and their own language.
  (9) Teachers should use their L1 for checking students' comprehension. This is essential because students' correct understanding of what's going on is necessary.

Where and How Can You Learn Classroom English?

- Where can you learn classroom English? Willis' (1981) book, *Teaching English through English*, includes useful classroom English expressions which you can use in preparing your lessons. As Willis puts it, her book is "designed to give you practice in effective use of classroom English and to extend your language teaching skills and techniques, with the aim of helping your students learn how to communicate successfully in English" (p. v). The book also gives you information on how to use social, personal and organizational English in classroom situations.

- *A Handbook of Classroom English,* written by Hughes (1981), *Classroom Language,* written by Salaberri (1995), and *Classroom English,* written by Gardner and Gardner (2000), provide us with both the language required by the teacher in the management of EFL classes and the strategies for effective use of that language.
- How can you learn classroom English expressions? Here are some methods:

  (1) Get lists of English expressions grouped around main situations and activities. The headings are usually grouped under language functions such as giving instructions, asking for information, classroom management, etc.
  (2) Choose two or three English expressions from each heading. However, remember that the choice made by each teacher is a personal decision and it will ultimately depend on your own pReferences and Additional Resources.

  e.g.,
  - Greeting: Hello, class. How are you?
  - Starting a lesson: Now, let's start our lesson.
  - Finding the page to study: Take out your books. Where did we stop last time?

  (3) Read the expressions aloud a couple of times and practice them alone or with a partner.

- Remember that you should practice classroom English expressions a lot. As a teacher trainee, you may benefit from some choral repetition of short phrases and sentences. Keep in mind that you should focus not only on the pronunciation of the words and sentences, but also on the stress and intonation.
- Recording yourself on a tape recorder can help you improve your English pronunciation as well as your confidence in using classroom English. Before preparing for the recording, you need to organize your practice plan. This plan contains the words and expressions you should record, listen to and evaluate.
- It is very useful for you to practice classroom English expressions in small groups. For example, you may work in groups of three or four as follows:

(1) Each member of a group is assigned a different role to play: a teacher, a secretary, a child (or children).
(2) The "teacher" teaches some English phrases (e.g., Repeat after me. Say it again. Good!).
(3) The "child" does what the "teacher" asks him to do.
(4) The "secretary" writes down what the "teacher" says.
(5) When the practice session is over, you may evaluate your joint effort.
(6) Switch roles and start a new session.

Task 2: Practice

1. Work in pairs. Write down appropriate expressions for the following functions and practice them.

   (1) Greeting the students
   (2) Finishing a class
   (3) Getting other people's attention
   (4) Asking for help
   (5) Asking for repetition

2. Each of the following English expressions is grammatically incorrect. Correct it with your partner. [The data are from *Elementary English Textbook 3, Teacher's Guide* (Ministry of Education, 2002).]

   (1) Let's look at the dialogue 1.
   (2) Let's role-play with your group.
   (3) Let's switch the role.

3. ESL experts recommend that the teacher use simple English (e.g., simple instructions, simple questions, etc.) so that every student can understand. Simplify the following expressions. [The data are from *Elementary English Textbook 3, Teacher's Guide* (Ministry of Education, 2002).]

   (1) Let me show you how to play the game.
   (2) Take a guess at what food I like.

(3) Can you guess what they talked about?
(4) Is there any reason that Nami likes summer?

4. Mr. Kim, an English teacher, wants his students to understand each of the following pictures, so he asks them the question, "What's happening?" What answers might he get from his students? Do you think his question is a good one for this activity? If not, how would you improve the activity? [The data are from *Elementary English Textbook 3, Teacher's Guide* (Ministry of Education, 2002).]

(1) Picture 1: A monkey in a tree is eating an apple.
(2) Picture 2: A fox jumps up to pick an apple, but fails to do it.
(3) Picture 3: The fox says to the monkey, "I don't like apples."
(4) Picture 4: The monkey picks an apple, throws it to the fox, and the fox says, "Thank you."

How to Teach Classroom English to Students

- How much English should you use in the classroom? The amount of classroom English used will depend on such factors as the level of the class, the length of the English learning period, the types of current learning activities, and the confidence and language ability of the teacher (Brewster et al. 1991, p. 188). If you teach a beginner-level class of young children, you will have to use simple instructions, greetings, questions, and comments in your English lessons.

- Gardner and Gardner (2000, p. 6-17) pose the following questions and give us some tips on how to teach classroom English to our students:

(1) Should I use classroom English right from the first lesson? The answer to this question is yes. You may give a few simple instructions, greetings, and comments in English from very early in the course. However, remember that you may give many other instructions in your learners' first language, particularly at the beginning of your English course.

(2) How much classroom English should I introduce in a lesson? In planning your lesson, you should make your decisions about the following:

- First, decide what classroom language to use and when to use it.
- Second, decide which expressions are simple and could be voiced in English.
- Third, decide which expressions are more difficult and need to be in your own language.
- When you have made these decisions, remember that you need to make a note of these choices.

(3) On the other hand, you will have to use your students' native language when,

- you provide an activity which may be too complicated to explain in English,
- you talk about life in an English-speaking country (a long story),
- you check that your learners have understood your instructions in English.

(4) What kind of classroom English expressions should I use in the lesson? It is desirable that you use English for the simple instructions, questions, and comments. First of all, you need to decide how many instructions in English will be enough for the beginner-level class of young children. Three to five simple instructions may be enough for the class. You can give all the other instructions in your own language. Of course, you may introduce in English a few questions and comments, in addition to the three to five instructions.

(5) There are some possible answers to the question, "What kind of instructions should I give in English during the lesson?" First of all, choose instructions which you will use frequently (You answer). Second, choose instructions the meaning of which can be shown with actions (Quiet). Third, choose instructions that are at the beginning of a sequence (I'll show you how to play). Fourth, choose instructions which are very different from one another (Sit down, Stand up).
(6) At what points in the lesson should I introduce new classroom English expressions? Do not teach all the new English expressions you have chosen at the same point in the lesson. Teach each expression at a different time during the lesson.
(7) How should I teach classroom English to the learners? First, try to make the meaning of the new expression clear; then practice it with your learners. Various teaching materials and techniques (e.g., hand movements, pictures, videos) can be used.

Task 3: Reflect

- Here are some guidelines on classroom English use. Put these in the order of their importance or value. Work in groups or pairs.

(1) Use classroom English in meaningful context.
(2) Use non-verbal elements such as gesture, mime, intonation, and facial expression.
(3) Use English for class routines which are necessarily repeated.
(4) Teach whole phrases, not just the words.
(5) Teach the language which is useful for interaction in group and pair work, games and interaction between the students and yourself.
(6) Keep your English simple, but natural.
(7) Use your classroom language consistently all through the course.
(8) Repeat the same expression if the students don't understand its meaning. Try to use the same expression during several lessons.

Task 4: Practice

- It is necessary that the teacher combine her English statements with actions when teaching children. Look at the following three examples and practice them with your partner.

Example 1: Telling a Story

Step 1: Presentation. The teacher tells a story with drawings or symbols on the board.

TEACHER'S WORDS	SYMBOLS
We are in Africa. We want to catch a lion. We are going on a lion hunt. Off we go!	
First we go along the street.	
Then we go over the bridge.	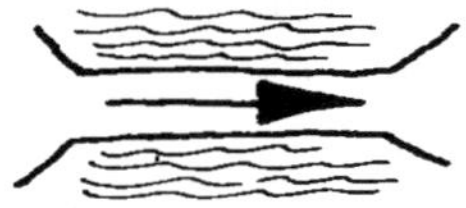
Next we go up the hill.	
Then we go down the hill.	
Next we go across the swamp.	
Now we go through the long grass ...	

Wait a minute, what's this? It has four legs. It has a long tail.
It has a big head. Help! It's the lion! Let's go back. Quick!

Now we go back the way we came – but fast!
(Students practice the key phrases)

Through the long grass.
Across the swamp.
Up the hill.
Down the hill.
Over the bridge.
Along the street.
Home! Hooray!

Step 2: Telling the Story. Now the teacher tells the story again. This time, she asks the class to follow her actions.

TEACHER'S WORDS	TEACHER'S ACTIONS
We are going on a lion hunt. Off we go!	
First we go along the street.	Make walking noises on your knees with your hands, left, right, left, right.
Then we go over the bridge.	'Walk' on the desk to make the hollow sound of the bridge.
Next we go up the hill. Slow down, it's a steep hill!	
Then we go down the hill.	Speed up.
Next we go across the swamp.	Make squelchy noises and lift your hands as if lifting them from something sticky.
Now we go through the long grass ...	Part the long grass with your arms, making swishing noises.
Wait a minute, what's this? It has four legs. It has a long tail.	Feel each leg. Feel the tail.

It has a big head. Help! It's the lion! Let's go back. Quick!	Feel the head.

Now go back the way you came.

Through the long grass.
Across the swamp.
Up the hill.
Down the hill.
Over the bridge.
Along the path.

Home! Hooray!	Slump in your chair and wave your hand in victory.

Step 3: Practice. Now a student comes to the front and tells the story. The other students help with actions and sounds. Then the students work in groups and practice the same story.

Example 2: Matching Cards

- Materials: picture cards, word cards

TEACHER'S WORDS	TEACHER'S ACTIONS
Today we are going to play a game called "remember." (Say the word game in L1 if necessary.)	Holds up large matching pictures and word cards and emphasizes the word "remember."
Look.	Places 6 large cards face down on a flannel board on the wall.
I need a partner. Who will help me?	Gestures to the class and picks a child who has volunteered.
Thank you. Anna. Now it's my turn. I take two cards. I turn over the cards.	Points to herself as she says "It is my turn." Takes two cards from the flannel board and turns them over slowly and shows them to the students.

What is this picture? And what is this word?	Points to one card which shows the picture of "an ice cream cone" and then to the other which shows the word "cake." Looks at Anna and the other students encouragingly to see if they can answer.
The picture is an ice cream cone. The word is cake.	Points to each card as she speaks.
Do they match? No, they don't match.	Looks at the students inquiringly. Points to the picture and to the word card and shakes her head as she says "They don't match."
Now I put the cards back in the same place.	Places the cards back on the flannel board in the same place.
Now it is your turn, Anna. Take two cards. Turn them over. What is this picture? Anna: Cake. What is this word? Anna: Cake.	Gestures to show the pupil what to do; gets the pupil to show the cards to the class, points to a picture of a cake and then points to the word card "cake."
Do they match? Anna: Match. Yes, they match. You have one set.	Points to the two cards and asks Anna if they match and then gives Anna the two cards.
Now it is my turn. I take two cards. I turn them over.	Takes two cards and turns them over.
This is an ice cream cone. This word is ice cream cone.	Points to the cards as she says the words and encourages the students to say the words with her.

Do they match? Pupils: Match.	Looks at the students inquiringly for an answer.
That's right. They match. Now I have one set.	
Now who wants to play?	Gestures to the class and picks another student who repeats the activity.
Let's play in groups this time.	Divides the class into groups and gives a set of cards to each group.

Example 3: Making a Fortune Teller

Step 1: Demonstrating how to make a fortune teller

TEACHER'S WORDS　　　　TEACHER'S ACTIONS

Now watch carefully.

First, fold your paper like this.
Press hard (with your thumb) like this.

Now, open your paper again.

Next, turn it round.
Now fold it like this.

Open it.
Now, watch!

Fold it like this.
Press hard with your thumb.

And fold it like this ... press hard

And fold it like this ... press hard

And fold it like this ... press hard

Now watch carefully.
Turn it over like this.

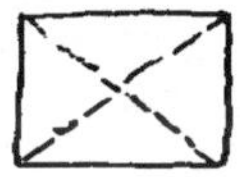

Next, fold it like this ...
press hard.

Now like this ... press hard.

Then like this ... press hard.

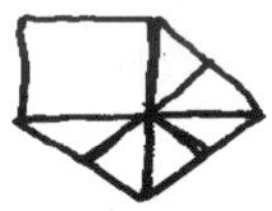

Then like this.

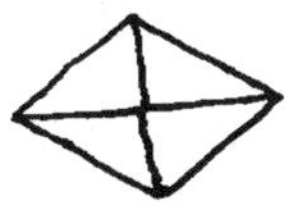

Next, fold it like this.
Yes! Press hard.

Then like this......

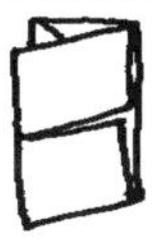

Now, watch ···
(The teacher demonstrates how the fortune teller works).

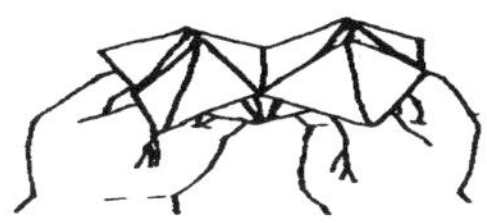

Step 2: Writing inside. The teacher writes four cities (e.g., Seoul, New York, London, Paris), and eight fortune words (e.g., famous, rich, poor, tall, teacher, doctor, president, big family) on the board. He asks children to write them on the flap like this:

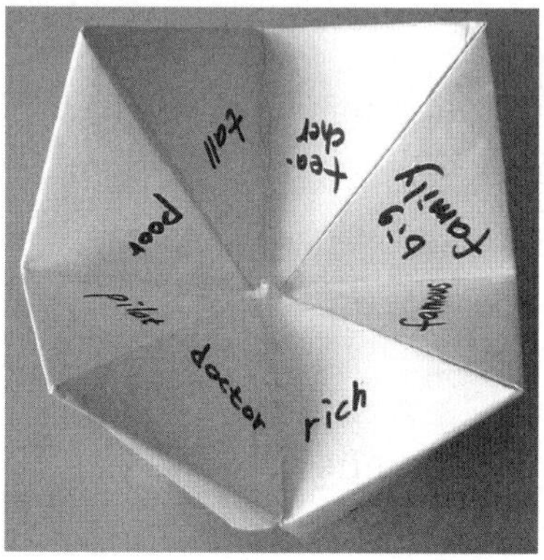

Step 3: Fortune telling. The teacher picks a student and shows the class how to play.

Teacher: Choose a city.
Child: Seoul.
Teacher: Say a number.
Child: Five.
Teacher: *(makes five moves with the fortune teller, counting)* One, two, three…
Teacher: You will be famous.

(The teacher divides the class into groups and gets them to play.)

Summary

1. ***Why Classroom English.*** Gardner and Gardner (2000) point out that you as well as your students get the following benefits from using English in class:
   (1) Learners recognize that the English lesson is quite different from other lessons such as social studies, history, math, etc.
   (2) Learners develop thinking skills in English.
   (3) Learners learn actively.
   (4) Learners gain confidence in replying to your instructions or questions.
   (5) You create a good English-speaking atmosphere.
   (6) You increase your own confidence as an EFL teacher by using English.

   Moon (2000, p. 63) also provides a list of the advantages of using English to teach English:
   (1) Students are exposed to more language input.
   (2) Students get confidence when replying to your instructions or questions.
   (3) Teaching in English provides real reasons for using English to communicate.
   (4) Students pick up much classroom language without their teacher's direct instruction.
   (5) Students are motivated to learn English actively.
   (6) Using English will help students develop thinking skills in English.
2. ***How to Learn Classroom English.*** How can you learn classroom English? You need lists of English expressions grouped around key situations and activities. Then, you choose two or three English phrases and list them under each heading. After choosing some basic English expressions, read them out aloud a couple of times for practice.

   Recording yourself on a tape recorder can help you improve your pronunciation in using classroom English. Before preparing for the recording, you need to organize your practice plan.
3. ***How to Teach Classroom English to Students.*** On this issue, Gardner and Gardner (2000) suggested these questions:
   (1) Should I use classroom English right from the first lesson?
   (2) How much classroom English should I introduce in a lesson?

(3) What kind of classroom English expressions should I use in the lesson?
(4) At what points in the lesson should I introduce new classroom English expressions?
(5) How should I teach a new classroom English expression?

Useful Internet Sites

1. Classroom English: Theory and Practice
   - http://www.finchpark.com
2. Boggle's World
   - http://www.bogglesworld.com

References and Additional Resources

Brewster, J., Ellis, G., & Girard, D. (1991). *The primary English teacher's guide.* London: Penguin Books.

Gardner, B., & Gardner, F. (2000). *Classroom English.* Oxford: Oxford University Press.

Halliwell, S. (1992). *Teaching English in the primary classroom.* London: Longman.

Hughes, G. S. (1981). *A handbook of classroom English.* Oxford: Oxford University Press.

Ministry of Education. (2002). *Elementary school English 3: Teacher's guide.* Seoul: Daehan Textbook Inc.

Ministry of Education. (2002). *Elementary school English 6: Teacher's guide.* Seoul: Daehan Textbook Inc.

Moon, J. (2000). *Children learning English.* Oxford: Macmillan Heinemann.

Salaberri, S. (1995). *Classroom language.* Oxford: Macmillan Heinemann.

Scott, W. A., & Ytreberg, L. H. (1990). *Teaching English to children.* London: Longman.

Willis, J. (1981). *Teaching English through English.* London: Longman.

Chapter 14
Songs and Games

Chapter Fourteen is presented to provide some songs and games which are designed to teach English to children. It also aims to offer some practical tips on how to use songs and games effectively in the classroom. Hence, there are three parts in this chapter: songs to motivate young learners to practice English, games to encourage the learners to use English for communication, and some tips on using songs and games for English classes. It should be noted that some of the previous chapters also include many games.

In this chapter, we will consider:
(1) Why are songs and games useful in teaching English to young learners?
(2) What are competitive games?
(3) How are competitive games different from cooperative games?
(4) How can we acquire feedback from students after song and game activities?

Songs

- Children love to sing. They like to make musical sounds and follow rhythm. Since singing songs is so much fun for them, children can easily remember what they hear and say while singing. Consequently, songs can be a very effective means of teaching English to young learners.
- There are several more reasons why songs are useful as:

① English is a stress-timed language. Children can naturally learn the rhythms of English through songs and chants.
② Songs are helpful for children to learn English sounds, stresses and accents.
③ With enough practice children can easily internalize English expressions. They can naturally learn by heart daily routine expressions and language chunks through songs and chants.
④ Because songs and chants provide natural and meaningful contexts, they are useful for learning words.

⑤ Songs and chants reduce learners' anxiety, making the learning less stressful.

- There are many different kinds of songs, from traditional nursery rhymes to instructive songs, which are specially designed to teach ESL/EFL. Traditional nursery rhymes have some old expressions which might be hard for EFL learners to understand. However, they are an important part of the life of English-speaking children. Hence, they are highly recommended for young EFL learners who will enjoy this element of English-speaking culture.
- Instructive songs are made mainly for teaching purposes. They are useful in practicing sentence patterns or certain kinds of vocabulary. For example, the song below is used to practice the sentence pattern, "Let's play ___," and sports vocabulary. By replacing the word 'basketball' with the names of other sports, children can practice the sentence pattern as well as the names of the sports.

Let's Play Basketball

- Some songs are good for singing and others are suitable for doing some actions while singing. The following are sample nursery rhymes, songs for singing and songs for both singing and actions:

1. Nursery Rhymes

(1) Please Porridge Hot,

Please porridge hot,
Please porridge cold,
Please porridge in the pot.
Nine days old.
Some like it hot,
Some like it cold,
Some like it in the pot
Nine days old.

(2) Baa, Baa, Black Sheep

Baa, Baa, Black Sheep
Have you any wool?
Yes sir, yes sir
Three bags full;
One for the master,
One for the dame,
And one for the little boy
Who lives down the lane.

(3) Hey Diddle Diddle

Hey diddle diddle
the cat and the fiddle
the cow jumped over the moon
The little dog laughed
to see such sport
and the dish
ran away with the spoon.

(4) Georgie Porgie, Pudding and Pie

Georgie Porgie, Pudding and Pie,
Kissed the girls and made them cry;
When the boys came out to play,
Georgie Porgie ran away.

(5) **Burnie Bee, Burnie Bee**

Burnie Bee, Burnie Bee
Tell me when your wedding be.
If it be tomorrow day,
Take your wings and fly away.

(6) **Jack and Jill**

Jack and Jill went up the hill
to fetch a pail of water;
Jack fell down and broke his crown,
And Jill came tumbling after.
Up got Jack, and home did trot,
As fast as he could caper,
To old Dame Dob, who patched his nob
With vinegar and brown paper.

2. Songs for Singing

(1) **Hickory, dickory, dock,**

Hickory, dickory, dock,
The mouse ran up the clock.
The clock struck one,
The mouse ran down,
Hickory, dickory, dock.

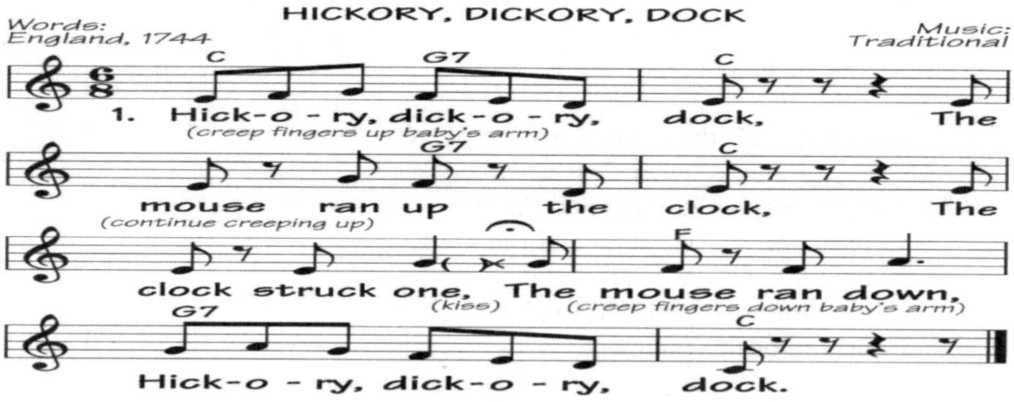

(2) A, B, C

A, B, C, tumble down D, The cat's in the cupboard and can't see me.

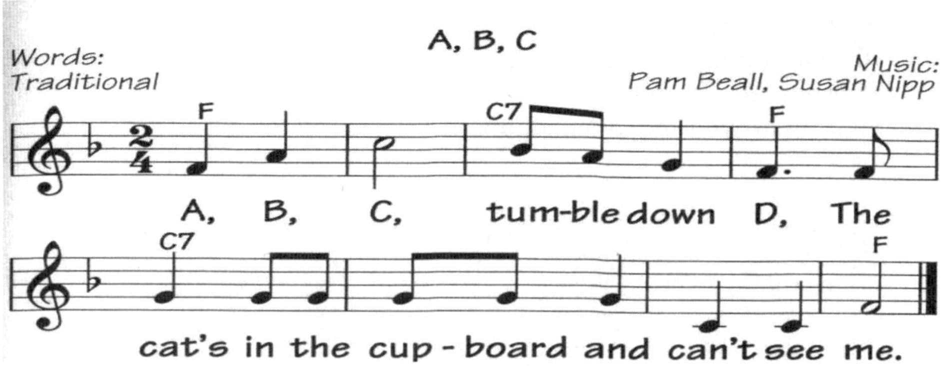

(3) Baby's clothes

Baby's wearing a red hat,

Red hat, red hat. Baby's wearing a red hat all day long.

(4) Baby bye

Baby bye, there's a fly,
We will watch him, you and I,
There he goes, on his toes,
Right up to your nose, nose, nose.

(5) The family

This is mama, kind and dear; This is papa, standing near,
This is brother, see how tall; This is sister, not so tall.
This is baby, sweet and small. These are family one and all.

(6) Clap along with me

Clap, clap, clap your hands, clap along with me,
Clap, clap clap your hands, clap along with me.
Clap a little faster now, clap along with me,
Clap a little faster now, clap along with me.

3. Songs for Singing and Doing Actions

(1) Ring around the rosy

Ring around the rosy, a pocketful of posies, Ashes, ashes,
We all fall DOWN!

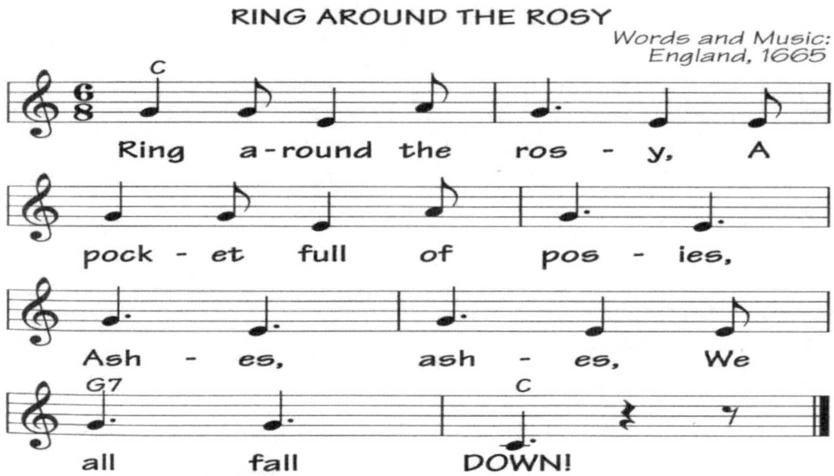

* Hold hands with students and move together in a large circle. Fall down on the last word, "Down."

(2) This is the way we take a bath

This is the way we take a bath,
Take a bath, take a bath,
This is the way we take a bath
Splish! Splish! Splash!

This is the way we wash our face,
Wash our face, wash our face,
This is the way we wash our face,
So early Monday morning.

This is the way we brush our teeth,
Brush our teeth, brush our teeth,
This is the way we brush our teeth

So early Tuesday morning.

This is the way we comb our hair,
Comb our hair, comb our hair,
This is the way we comb our hair
So early Wednesday morning.

This is the way we button our shirt,
Button our shirt, button our shirt,
This is the way we button our shirt
So early Thursday morning.

This is the way we tie our shoes,
Tie our shoes, tie our shoes,
This is the way we tie our shoes
So early Friday morning.

This is the way we put on our coats
Put on our coats, put on our coats,
This is the way we put on our coats
So early Saturday morning.

Here we go round the mulberry bush
The mulberry bush, the mulberry bush,
Here we go round the mulberry bush,
So early Sunday morning.

* Act out the words while singing the song.

(3) Where is Thumbkin?

Where is Thumbkin, where is Thumbkin?
Here I am, here I am.
How are you today, sir?
Very well, I thank you.
Run away, run away.

Where is Pointer, where is Pointer?
Here I am, here I am.
How are you today, sir?
Very well, I thank you.
Run away, run away.

Where is Tall Man, where is Tall Man?
Here I am, here I am.
How are you today, sir?
Very well, I thank you.
Run away, run away.

Where is Pinkie, where is Pinkie?
Here I am, here I am.
How are you today, sir?

Very well, I thank you.
Run away, run away.

Where are all the men, where are all the men?
Here we are, here we are.
How are you today, sirs?
Very well, we thank you.
Run away, run away.

- Make two fists and put them behind your back. When you sing, "Here I am," bring out your right fist and hold up your thumb. Then do the same with your left fist. When you sing, "How are you today, sir?" wiggle your right thumb. For "Very well, I thank you," wiggle your left thumb. On "Run away," put your right fist and then your left fist behind your back. Do the same thing for each of your fingers. For "all the men," use all of your fingers.

(4) Bingo

There was a farmer had a dog.
And Bingo was his name, O!
B, I, N, G, O, B, I, N, G, O, B, I, N, G, O.
And Bingo was his name, O!

* First sing the song through. As you sing the song the second time, clap your hands once instead of singing the letter "B." The third time, clap for "B" and "I"; the fourth time for "B," "I," and "N"; and so forth until you clap for all the letters.

(5) Head and shoulders

Head and shoulders, knees and toes, knees and toes, knees and toes,
Head and shoulders, knees and toes, eyes, ears, mouth and nose.

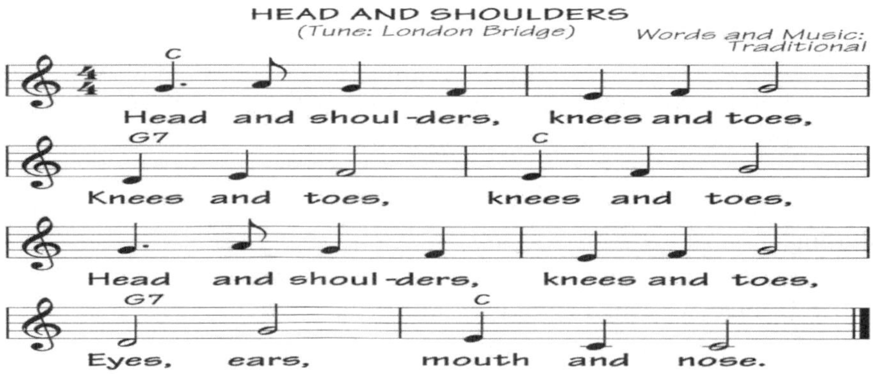

* As you sing the song, simply point to the appropriate body part.

(6) One elephant went out to play

One elephant went out to play, out on a spider's web one day.
He had such enormous fun. He called for another elephant to come.

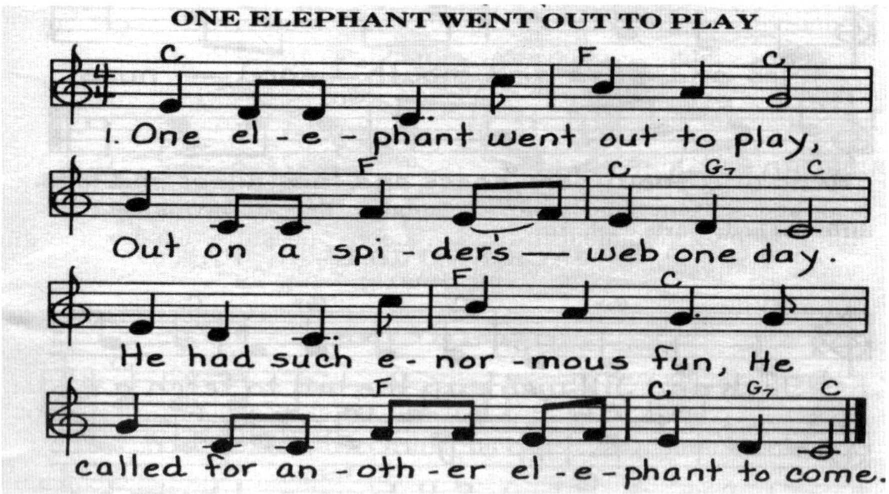

* While all the students are singing, a student walks around a room imitating an elephant. At the end of the song, he/she chooses another 'elephant' to follow him/her and the students repeat the song. At the end of each repetition, the last 'elephant' chooses another new 'elephant' to follow him/her.

Games

- There are generally two kinds of games: competitive games and cooperative games. In competitive games, players or teams race to be the first or to be winners. In cooperative games, players work together to reach a common goal (e.g., solving problems).
- It needs to be noted that cooperative games, when they are used with some

caution, could boost young learners' real desire to communicate with others in English. On the other hand, the competitive element or the speed of competitive games might distort the actual purpose of English activities - learning English. Especially when children focus more on winning the games than on learning English, become too heated, or get out of control, the games might not encourage them to practice English.

1. Cooperative Games

1) **Information gap games**: In these games, one student has some information which his/her partner doesn't have. They need to talk a lot to share the information.

(1) Who is this person?

① The teacher keeps a picture of a person who is famous locally, nationally, or internationally.
② One student from each group comes to the teacher's desk to see the picture and goes back to his/her group.
③ The remaining members of each group ask questions to guess whose picture is on the teacher's desk.

Expressions to practice:
Is it a boy/girl?, Is it he or she?, Do you like him/her?, What does he/she do?, Where is he/she from?, Is he/she Korean, Is he/she Japanese?, Is he/she Chinese?, Is he/she tall?, Is he/she smart?....

(2) Find the differences

① Looking at two similar pictures, you and your partner find the differences between the two pictures.
② You can't compare the two pictures by putting them side by side. You can look at only your picture while your partner looks at his/hers.
③ Describe your picture to your partner to find differences.

(3) **Read my lips**

① Read the words on the word cards silently.

② Your team members should read your lips. No sounds, please.

(4) **Vocabulary game 1**

① Draw pictures without speaking.

② Your team members guess what you are drawing only by looking at the picture as you draw.

(5) **Vocabulary game 2**

① You answer questions about a word on a word card.

② Your team members ask only yes/no questions to get clues to guess the word correctly.

(6) **Vocabulary game 3**

① You answer the questions about the words on the word cards.

② Your team members ask only WH questions this time.

2) **A Class survey**

(1) You ask your classmates what sports they like, and fill in a questionnaire grid like this:

Sports	Do you like ______?	Total
Football	1 1 1 1 1	5
Baseball		
Swimming		
Skiing		

(2) You ask your classmates whether they live in an apartment or in a house to fill in the following grid:

Do you live in a/an______?

Name	Apartment	House
Yoomi		
Hyunsuk		
Meere		
Hana		

3) Hand-clapping games

(1) Who took the cookie from the cookie jar?

① All students: Who took the cookie from the cookie jar? Students slap their lap, clap hands, and snap the fingers on the left hand then the right hand following the rhythm. They repeat the hand clapping in rhythm (slap, clap, slap, clap, snap, pause, snap, pause -one beat pauses- repeat all) while playing this game.

② Leader: Sooni took the cookie from the cookie jar.
Sooni: Who me?
All students: Yes, you.
Sooni: Not me.
All students: Then who?
Sooni: Hanna took the cookie from the cookie jar.
Hanna: Who me?
(Repeat the chant and the hand motions)

(2) Here is the church

Here is the church (Clap both hands with fingers hiding inside),
and here is the steeple (Raise index fingers to form a point).
Open the doors (Move thumbs aside),
and here are the people (Open hands slightly, wiggle the fingers).
Close the doors (Return thumbs to closed position).
Where are the people? (Shrug the shoulders in puzzlement)
Open the doors (Move thumbs aside),
There go the people (Fingers walk away).

2. Competitive Games

1) Speed game

① Make a group of five.

② The first player of each group takes the leader's role by taking five animal word cards from the teacher. He describes them one by one to the other students.

③ Once the other group members guess the leader's five animals' names correctly, the next player takes the leader's role and describes the next five animals written on the next five animal word cards.

④ The first group, which guesses all five members' 25 animals' names fastest, becomes the winning team.

2) **Animal bingo**

① The students draw a bingo board with 16 boxes.
② The students write 16 animals' names on it.
③ The teacher calls out the names of the animals and the players look at their boards to see whether they have the name that is called.
④ If a "sheep" is called, they look for the word "sheep." If they have the word, they check the word; if they don't, they need to wait for the teacher's next word.
⑤ The first player to check four words in a row vertically, horizontally or diagonally raises his/her hand and says "Bingo." He/She is the winner.

3) **Time bingo**

Play bingo with clocks.

Tips on Using Songs and Games

1. Classroom Language

- The issue of the role of the mother tongue when learning a second/foreign language is still open to discussion. That is, the question of whether to use the Korean spoken/written language during English class is still being debated and it is not likely that we will soon see an answer to the question. However, many English teachers and researchers agree that it is essential to use as much English as possible during class even in elementary school; even though there are times when communication in the Korean language is strongly recommended.
- There are times when young learners are easily frustrated and become less focused; for example, if they listen to directions for an unfamiliar English activity entirely in English. Whenever the teacher is doubtful that his/her students are following, he/she is recommended to ask them some feedback questions (questions to check their understanding). Even when the students answer the questions in Korean, it is all right as long as their answers are right. Based on the answers the students give, the teacher can decide when to depend on Korean communication.

- Usually when the writer of this chapter was not sure of her young students' understanding, she wrote the numbers 1 to 5 on the blackboard and stood right in front of the number 1 saying "Yes, yes, yes I do understand," and raised her one hand. She stood in front of the number 2 saying, "Yes, yes, I understand"; the number 3 "Yes, I understand"; the number 4 "No, I don't understand"; the number 5 "No, no, I don't understand." Then, she asked the students to raise their hand when she stood in front of the number that represented their level of understanding. In this way, the writer tried her best not to depend on Korean speaking to communicate with her students.
- There are some guidelines concerning the language used during class:

  (1) Give clear directions on which language students should use, only English or Korean/English.
  (2) Speak easy English utterances clearly in order to be understood by the students.
  (3) Encourage the students to use English frequently.
  (4) Ignore the students' use of Korean for the sake of communication.

- One very effective way to encourage children to use English during English class is to put commonly used English expressions on the classroom walls. Korean translations may or may not be added to the English expressions. With the expressions on the wall, the teacher can point to an appropriate expression whenever one is needed.
- Another way for teachers to avoid speaking Korean during class is to appoint a student translator who helps the teacher by translating what the teacher says when the teacher asks him/her to do so. Since the English level of the student translator is highly advanced, he/she is easily bored and inattentive during English class. This is a wonderful way to help students, who have a highly advanced level of English, and other students at the same time.

2. Grouping

- In general, there are four ways to arrange your students when you play English games: individually, in pairs, in groups and as a whole class. For most reading and writing activities, individual work is recommended. Pair work works best in speaking activities, such as role-play games and information-gap games. It is a very good idea to ask a model pair to demonstrate what you want the children to do. Group activities are used quite often in communication-oriented activities. Groups of three or four seem to work best. Whole-class activities are effective when the teacher wants to teach something directly to the students or when the students make a presentation.

3. Feedback

- Getting feedback from students on an activity they have performed is an essential part of language learning or any kind of learning. Feedback can focus on: (1) the language points the students have been working on, and (2) the way the students have performed the tasks required for the activity. The older students and/or those with a higher English level can be asked to give their opinions about the suitability of a task used to practice a given language point. The simplest way to get students' feedback is to ask them to draw a sad, a normal or a happy face on their paper.

- Also, the teacher can draw a sad, a normal, and a happy face on the blackboard and then ask students which face describes their reaction toward a game or an activity they just did. Here is an example (Scott and Ytreberg, 1990).

- Based on the students' reaction, the teacher can plan the next activity. Reflection time is always needed; for students to think back about their performance and ways to perform better, and for the teacher to think about how to be of greater help to the students. Also, feedback activities are wonderful for young learners. It allows them to feel responsible for their own learning, that is, to be autonomous learners.

Summary

In this chapter, we have considered:

- ***Songs.*** Singing songs is a very effective way to teach children because they love to sing. While singing traditional nursery rhymes and instructive songs children can easily remember what they hear and speak, and they acquire English very naturally. Traditional nursery rhymes might be hard for young Korean students, but they are still recommended because students generally enjoy this element of English culture. Instructive songs are designed mainly for teaching sentence patterns or certain kinds of vocabulary.
- ***Games.*** Games are divided into competitive games and cooperative games. In competitive games, players or teams race to be the winner, while in cooperative games players work together to reach a common goal (e.g., solving problems). Both types of games need to be applied with some caution. Students might become too anxious to win when playing competitive games. They might not be challenged enough to win when playing cooperative games.

Useful Internet Sites

1. http://englishfork.com/main/index.php
2. http://www.wordpark.co.kr
3. http://www.littlefox.co.kr/index.htm,
4. http://www.zazajoy.com
5. http://jr.naver.com/English,
6. http://kr.kids.yahoo.com ,
7. http://old.edunet4u.net/edunetWebApp/jsp/student/study/cho_main.jsp
8. http://funschool.kaboose.com
9. http://www.funbrain.com
10. http://www.kids-space.org

11. http://disney.go.com/characters/today/index.html
12. http://barbie.everythinggirl.com
13. http://www.scholastic.com
14. http://www.nationalgeographic.com
15. http://www.eslkidstuff.com
16. http://www.abc.net/directory/Kids_and_Teens
17. http://www.bbc.co.uk/schools/laac/idex.shtml
18. http://www.storyplace.org
19. http://www.lil-fingers.com

References and Additional Resources

Beall, P. C., & Susan, H. N. (1977). *We sing children's songs and fingerplays.* Los Angeles: Price Stern Sloan.

Beall, P. C., & Susan, H. N. (1981). *We sing and play.* Los Angeles: Price Stern Sloan.

Beall, P. C., & Susan, H. N. (1990). *We sing sing-alongs.* Los Angeles: Price Stern Sloan.

Beall, P. C., & Susan, H. N. (1996). *We sing for baby.* Los Angeles: Price Stern Sloan.

Claire, E. (1988). *ESL teacher's activities kit.* Englewood Cliffs, New Jersey: Prentice Hall.

Hadfield, J. (1992). *Elementary communication games: A collection of games and activities for elementary students of English.* London: Nelson.

Murphey, T. (1992). *Music and song.* Oxford: Oxford University Press.

Oh, M. (1996). *English games for Korean elementary class.* Seoul: Hong-ik Media Ltd.

Oh, M. (1998) *Easy English games.* Seoul: Hong-ik Media Ltd.

Phillips. S. (1993). *Young learners.* Oxford: Oxford University Press.

Reichmeier, B. (1987). *Play-along and counting songs.* New York: Random House.

Chapter 15
Culture

Chapter Fifteen examines various aspects of teaching culture in the foreign language classroom. It first attempts to define culture in terms of language teaching. It also explores the why and how of teaching culture and provides a framework for this learning/teaching which should give you a lot of ideas about teaching culture in the English classroom.

In this chapter, we will consider:
(1) The meaning of culture.
(2) Reasons to teach culture.
(3) Goals for teaching culture.
(4) Identifying cultural information.
(5) How to incorporate culture into the foreign language classroom.
(6) A framework for learning/teaching culture.
(7) Some tips on teaching culture.

What Is Culture?

- Hymes (1996) emphasizes that the learning of culture is an integral part of language learning and education. This is because it crucially influences the values of the community, everyday interaction, the norms of speaking and behaving, and the sociocultural expectations of an individual's role.
- Curtain and Pesola (1994) mention that culture, empathy for other people, and global awareness are important elements in the teaching of foreign languages at the elementary school level. Culture has been interpreted by these linguists as:
  (1) the important names and places in the history, geography, and

literature of a people;
(2) their great works of art and music;
(3) knowledge of getting along in the day-to-day life of a people.

1. Visible Culture vs. Invisible Culture

- In EFL/ESL teaching, culture refers to distinctly different domains of people's lives. Some scholars classify culture into two forms: visible and invisible.

  1) **Visible culture:** The visible aspects of culture are readily apparent to anyone and can be discussed and explained relatively easily. Examples are:
     ① the literature, the arts, the architecture, and the history of a particular people;
     ② the style of dress, cuisine, customs, festivals, and other traditions

  2) **Invisible culture:** Most people are not even aware of the invisible aspects of culture. For example, North Americans have their own sociocultural norm, worldview, beliefs and assumptions.

- Scollon and Scollon (1995) state that the culturally determined concepts of what is acceptable, appropriate, and expected in one's behavior is acquired during the process of socialization. For example, in the classroom, the roles of the student and the teacher are defined by the sociocultural values of the larger community and the society. Students from one culture may easily speak up in front of their classmates, whereas students from another culture may have trouble doing the same.
- As Byram and Morgan (1994) point out, "learners cannot simply shake off their own culture and step into another … their culture is a part of themselves .... as social beings …"

2. Big Culture vs. little culture

- We also can think of culture at two different levels as identified by Brooks (1975): big culture and little culture.

1) **Big Culture (Big C)**

① Big culture covers a nation's international institutions which organize and supervise the life of a community. So, political, religious, educational, military, sporting, artistic and scientific institutions are all examples of Big Culture.

② There are colorful and exciting ceremonies associated with big culture. These are often the only way to interest younger students in big culture. As adults we all agree that the Constitution of the United States is a remarkable document, but can we make it 'interesting' to 12 year olds who understand little about the constitution of their own country?

2) **little culture (little c)**

① Little culture is the lifestyle of the ordinary people. What are their houses like? What do they eat? What do they do in their spare time?

② Since students live within their own little culture, they know about their own. Hence they have a context with which to compare the information about little culture in a different place.

③ In general, we should concentrate on the aspects of little culture (particularly as it applies to their own age group) until the students begin to learn about their own big culture.

Why Do We Teach Culture?

- We teach about foreign cultures in order to broaden our students' outlook on the world and to develop their understanding of the wider world. But what do we give them to do this? Facts.
- Facts alone do not bring understanding. We must 'engage' with those facts and have some emotional reactions to them.

1. Differences and Similarities

- When we select topics from big culture or from little culture, we often select the topics which show the greatest differences between our own culture and the foreign culture. We seem to think that differences are more interesting than similarities.

2. Emotional Response

- When we give information (facts) to our students, we should not simply ask them to absorb and remember that information. We should invite them to 'feel' something about that information. We should not expect them to like everything about the foreign culture. The initial reaction to a foreign culture is very often negative (even amongst adults).

3. From Understanding to Tolerance

- As our students' understanding of a foreign culture develops, we should hope that this understanding will bring tolerance. Tolerance means accepting and allowing the behavior of other people, 'providing they stay in their foreign countries'. But at this stage, there is no willingness to investigate and enjoy the delights of the foreign culture.

4. From Tolerance to Celebration

- But 'tolerance' is not enough. We need to lead our students from tolerating cultural differences to celebrating their rich variety.

5. Patriotism and Celebration

- Learning to understand and enjoy a foreign culture should also lead to a more mature understanding and appreciation of the home culture. An 'international citizen' is not a person with no home culture but a person who loves their home culture whilst celebrating the cultural diversity which is offered by the world.

Goals for Teaching Culture

- Ned Seelye (1988) provides a framework for facilitating the development of cross-cultural communication skills. The following goals are a modification of Seelye's 'seven goals of cultural instruction':

1) To help students develop an understanding of the fact that all people exhibit culturally-conditioned behavior.

   Example: When talking with one another, speakers in many Asian countries stand much closer to one another than is common in the United States.

2) To help students develop an understanding that social variables such as age, sex, social class, and place of residence influence the way in which people speak and behave.

   *Example: In German-speaking countries, children address their peers and immediate family members with the familiar form "**du**," and all other adults with the formal second-person form "**Sie**." In Korea, people address one another differently depending on their relationship to one another and their social status.*

3) To help students become more aware of conventional behavior in common situations in the target culture.

   Example: Individuals in many European countries habitually shake hands when they meet one another on the street. In Korea a bow is a part of every greeting, and in South America a greeting is often accompanied by a hug.

4) To help students increase their awareness of the cultural connotation of certain words and phrases in the target culture.

Example: Pigs and white horses are associated with good luck in Germany. Spiders are considered a sign of good fortune in Japan.

5) To help students use supporting evidence to evaluate and refine generalizations about the target culture.

   Example: Americans visiting a German home sometimes conclude that their hosts are unfriendly because they keep the doors between rooms closed all the time. Germans, by contrast, feel their American guests are disorderly because they leave doors open.

6) To help students develop the necessary skills to locate and organize information about the target culture.

   Example: Children often have questions about house pets, school schedules, allowances, and common aspects of daily life in the target culture.

7) To stimulate students' intellectual curiosity about the target culture, and to encourage empathy towards its people.

   Example: All activities that bring the child into contact with individuals living in or otherwise representing the target culture provide an opportunity for development toward this goal.

- Tomalin & Stempleski (1993) recommend that these goals be incorporated into the following practical teaching principles.

  1) Access the culture through the language being taught.
  2) Make the study of cultural behavior an integral part of each lesson.
  3) Aim for students at all levels to achieve cross-cultural understanding-awareness of their own culture, as well as that of the culture which uses the target language.
  4) Recognize that teaching about culture does not necessarily imply a need for behavioral change, but merely an awareness and tolerance of the cultural influences affecting one's own and others' behavior.

Identifying Cultural Information

- It is not easy to select and use cultural items to teach English. Following Pesola's (1991) categorization of culture will help. Pesola identifies culture in terms of cultural symbols, cultural products, and cultural practices. Some examples follow:

1. Cultural Symbols

(1) flags, insignia related to children's interests
(2) significant national or geographic monuments
(3) symbols associated with holidays
(4) symbols of good and bad luck
(5) symbolic meaning of certain animals
(6) heroes from history or myth

2. Cultural Products

(1) significant examples of the visual arts (and artists)
(2) significant examples of the musical arts (and composers)
(3) important characters, events, and themes from folk literature
(4) traditional children's songs, rhymes, and games
(5) traditional stories and legends
(6) examples of folk art
(7) currency and coins, stamps, and other realia
(8) traditional and holiday foods

3. Cultural Practices

(1) forms of greeting
(2) celebration of holidays
(3) use of gestures
(4) meals and eating practices
(5) shopping
(6) favorite playtime and recreational activities

(7) home and school life
(8) patterns of politeness
(9) types of pets and attitudes toward pets
(10) how children and families move from place to place

- These items could serve as the starting point of a thematic unit or as components of instruction. Children's literature - folk and fairy tales, contemporary children's books, songs, and rhymes - is a valuable resource of cultural information.

How to Incorporate the Study of Culture into the Language Classroom

- Better international understanding is a noble aim, but how can the transition be made from theoretical matters in an active, crowded, and sometimes noisy foreign language classroom? For teachers, challenge in all classroom work is the involvement of students' interest, attention, and active participation. Learning activities which focus on active rather than passive learning are the best.
- Traditional methods of teaching culture in the foreign language classroom have focused on formal culture and passive learning. Students do need both a geographical and historical perspective in order to understand contemporary behavior patterns but this can be done with hands-on activities. Beginning foreign language students want to feel, touch, smell, and see the people from foreign lands and not just hear their language. These are some ways to incorporate culture in English classroom:

1. Cultural Islands

- From the first day of class the teacher should have a cultural island in his/her classrooms. Posters, pictures, maps, signs, and realia of many kinds are essential in helping students develop a mental image. Assigning students foreign names from the first day can heighten students' interest. Short presentations on a topic of interest with appropriate pictures or slides add to this mental image. Start students off by making them aware of the influence of various foreign cultures in their own country. Introduce students to the words in their language or the place-names in their country that have been borrowed from the English language. This helps students realize that they already know many words in the target language. Some of the foods students eat are another example of the influence of a foreign culture.

2. Celebrating Festivals

- Celebrating foreign festivals is a favorite activity of many students. Even though this activity takes a lot of planning, it works well as a culminating activity. For example, some students start by bringing in some specific recipes and others put a cookbook together. Students then prepare for the festival by drawing posters, decorating the room, and preparing some of the foods in the cookbook. At Christmas time, it is good to learn some Christmas songs and poems. This kind of activity enables student to actively participate in the cultural heritage of the people they are studying.

3. Kinetics and Body Language

- Culture involves a network of verbal and non-verbal communication. If our goal is to teach communication, we must not neglect the most obvious form of non-verbal communication like gestures. A gesture, although learned, is largely an unconscious cultural phenomenon. Gestures convey the feel of the language to the student and when accompanied by verbal communication, inject greater authenticity into the classroom and make language study more interesting. It is suggested that teachers use foreign culture gestures when presenting dialogues, cuing students' responses, and helping students recall dialogue lines. At the beginning of the year, teachers can also show foreign films to students just to have them focus on body movements.

4. Culture Capsules

- Ursula Hendron (1980), in her article on teaching culture in the high school classroom, suggests using culture capsules. Culture capsules teach essential differences between American and foreign customs (related to dating, cuisine, pets, and sports) by comparing the two different cultures. The cultural insights from the culture capsule can be further illustrated by role playing. For example, Hendron (1980) suggests teaching dating customs in Spanish-speaking countries by creating an illusion of a plaza in the classroom with posters, props, music or slides. Students pretend to be young Latin-Americans and act out a Sunday paseo.

5. Raising Cross-Cultural Awareness

- Attitude is another factor in language learning that leads to cross-cultural understanding. It is said that the totality of language learning is comprised of three integrated components: linguistic, cultural, and attitudinal.
- As foreign language teachers, we all teach the basic sounds, vocabulary, and syntax of the target language, but do we recognize the value of teaching about a foreign culture? The most important long-term benefit from teaching culture is that learners gain the tools that will allow them to achieve their academic, professional, social and personal goals and become successful in their daily functioning in an EFL environment.

A Framework for Learning/Teaching Culture

- Patrick Moran (2001), an American teacher, devised a chart that can be used for teaching culture. It includes four components: 'knowing about', 'knowing how', 'know why' and 'knowing oneself.' It was basically designed to teach American culture, but it could be applied to the teaching of other cultures as well.

1. Knowing about (getting information)

(1) Nature of content - getting information:
   ① What is the capital of the US?
   ② Sports play an important role in American life.

(2) Learning objectives: demonstrate a mastery of the information.

(3) Techniques/activities : cultural readings; films/videotapes, recordings, realia (cultural artifacts), personal anecdotes.

(4) Note:
How culture is traditionally taught - giving students information and asking them to show that they know it. Teacher's role is an informant.

2. Knowing how (developing behaviors)

(1) Nature of content – skills:
① Buying tickets to a sports event.
② Cheering for your team at a football game.
③ Acting and speaking like American sports fans.

(2) Learning objectives: demonstrate an ability - fluency, expertise, confidence, ease.

(3) Techniques/activities: dialogs, role plays, simulations, field experiences.

(4) Note:
Where communicative competence in the language and culture occurs, students know both what to say and how to say it in a culturally appropriate manner. Teacher's role is a coach or model.

3. Knowing why (discovering explanations)

(1) Nature of content - values and assumptions:

① Why are sports so important to Americans?
② Are you making an observation or an interpretation?
③ Why do Americans have sports rituals?
④ How does this compare with your culture?
⑤ Demonstrate an ability, to infer, to generalize, to suspend judgment.
⑥ Curiosity, tolerance, sensitivity, empathy.

(2) Techniques/activities:

① Learners interpret and make explanations based on the above activities;
② Comparisons with their own culture;
③ Ethnography;
④ Reflective writing.

(3) Note:
Learners engage in actively using their powers of induction, analysis and intuition to draw conclusions about cultural information or experiences - like anthropologists. Teacher's role is a co-researcher or guide.

4. Knowing oneself (personalizing knowledge)

(1) Nature of content - self-awareness:
① What is the importance of sports in your life?
② How did it feel to act like Americans at a football game?
③ Would you choose this behavior for your own?

(2) Learning objectives: Through behavior/statements demonstrate an understanding of the feelings, values, opinions, and attitudes exhibited by another culture, and act upon them.

(3) Techniques/activities:
① Learners examine and make statements about themselves;
② Reflective writing;
③ Feedback on the above activities.

(4) Note:
Learners themselves are the subject matter in the process of guided self-discovery, as they study their own values and their reaction to the values exhibited by another culture. They decide whether or not to readjust their own values. Teacher's role is a counselor or guide.

Tips on Teaching Culture

- Elementary school English teachers who want to provide cultural experiences for their classes are constantly in search of authentic games, music, crafts, foods, and customs to share with their students. The following activities will help teachers achieve the cultural goals mentioned above:

(1) Invite foreign visitors or target-language speakers to visit the class and share their experiences, using visuals, slides, and as many concrete materials as possible.
(2) Learn and perform folk dances, sing songs and play games from the target culture.
(3) Encourage students to skim target-language newspapers or magazines to find pictures to illustrate concepts they are learning in class.
(4) Tell or read fables, folktales, and legends that come from the target culture or from other cultures around the world.
(5) Read to students from picture books written for children in the target culture and reflecting that culture.
(6) Use collections of games from around the world to locate suitable games played in the target culture, and incorporate these into units and lessons.

Task1: Reflect

1. Review the section "Goals for Teaching Culture" and identify five examples of culturally conditioned behavior (Cultural Goal 1) or conventional behavior (Cultural Goal 3) that are representative of the target culture you teach. Discuss how you might build these into the experiences of your elementary school English class.

2. Together with a classmate develop an inventory of cultural symbols, cultural products, and cultural practices.

3. You have invited a native speaker to speak to your English class of fifth-graders. Based on what you know about Korean language and culture, what instructions and advice will you give your speaker in advance?

Activities for Teaching Culture

<Activity 1>

Telephoning in the Target Culture

Objective: Students learn and practice telephoning in a target language (TL).

Materials:

1. Play/toy telephones
2. Audio or videotape of TL speakers talking on the phone
3. A text of the conversations (with blanks for students to fill in)

Activity:

1. Have learners listen to the model telephone conversations.
2. As they listen a second time, have them fill in the blanks.
3. Divide the students into pairs and have them place their chairs back-to-back to practice the dialogue.
4. Once they have mastered the language and conventions of telephone talk, have them improvise another conversation. If the first conversation involved making plans, make the second one about gossiping or asking for information.
5. Discuss similarities and differences in telephone talk between the target culture and home culture.
6. As homework, have students write up, in the target language, a telephone dialogue that they have had recently in their own language.

<Activity 2>

Making Cultural Inferences Using Currency

Objective:

Students explore cultural icons and symbols with a hands-on discovery project.

Materials:

1. Korean paper money and coins (or color photocopies)
2. US bills and coins (or color photocopies)
3. Short descriptions of the figures and/or symbols students will find on the currency. You should be able to find these fairly easily on the Internet
4. A graphic organizer that allows learners to compare US currency with Korean currency

Activity:

1. Divide the class into small groups and provide each group with some US money.
2. Have them discuss the shape, color, style, images and anything else they find significant. Have learners write down what they can infer about the US money.
3. Give students the descriptions and have them reflect on why these people and images have been chosen to represent the US culture. Ask them to consider whether heroes are the same across cultures.
4. Distribute the Korean currency. Have students complete the comparative chart and then discuss their findings as a class.
5. As homework, have students write up the comparisons in a short essay.

<Activity 3>

April Fool's Day

The Story

1. The first day of April is full of fun. It is April Fool's Day.
2. A fool is a person who does not think carefully. A fool easily believes things that are not true.
3. On April Fool's Day, people tell lies to fool other people. They play tricks. Then everyone laughs.

4. You can tell a lie on April Fool's Day. If someone believes the lie, say, "April Fool!"
5. Be careful. Someone may tell you a lie. If you believe it, they will say, "April fool!"
6. Here are some April Fool's Day lies for beginners.
   (1) "Your shoe is untied."
   (2) "There's a bug on your shoulder."
   (3) "There's a spot on your shirt."
   (4) "We're having a test this afternoon."
   (5) "I'm moving away next week."
7. You can play an April Fool's Day trick: You need a coin or a dollar, tape, and thread. Tape a very long thread to the money. Put the money down on the floor or the sidewalk. Hold the other end of the thread. Stand away. When someone sees the money and tries to pick it up, quickly pull the thread. Laugh and say, "April Fool!"

Questions

1. Do you know these words? Find the words in the story. Draw a line under them. Copy the words. Write the meanings.

lie/lies	fun	careful/carefully
believes	laughs	untied
flat	bill	trick
sidewalk	thread	pick it up

2. Answer:
   (1) What day is April Fool's Day? ______________________________
   (2) A fool is a person who easily believes things that are not ____.
   (3) On April Fool's Day, people tell ________ to fool other people.
   (4) If someone believes a lie on April Fool's Day, you say, "_________________!"
   (5) What are some April Fool's Day lies you can tell to trick people?
   ____
   ____
   ____
   ____
   ____

3. Discuss:
   (1) Do you celebrate April Fool's Day in your country?
   (2) Is there any other day when people play tricks on each other?
   (3) What kinds of lies are not funny on April Fool's Day?

Useful Internet Sites

1. http://teflchina.org/teach/culture
2. http://www.peacecorps.gov/wws/culturematters
3. http://www.ohiou.edu/esl/etc/student.html
4. http://www.lib.utexas.edu/maps/
5. http://www.behindthename.com

References and Additional Resources

Brooks, N. (1968). Teaching culture in the foreign language classroom. *Foreign Language Annals, 16,* 204-217.

Byram, M., & Morgan, C. (1994). *Teaching and learning and culture.* Clevedon, UK: Multilingual Matters.

Claire, E. (1990). *ESL Teacher's holiday activities kit.* West Nyack, New York: The Center for Applied Research in Education.

Curtain, H. A., & Pesola, A. (1994). *Languages and children: Making the Match.* White Clains, New York: Longman.

Hendon, U. S. (1980). Introducing culture in the high school foreign language class. F*oreign Language Annals, 13.* New York: ACTFL.

Hymes, D. (1996). *Ethnography, linguistics, narrative inequality.* Bristol, PA: Taylor and Francis.

Kramsch, C. J. (1983). Culture and constructs: Communicating attitudes and values in the foreign language classroom. *Foreign Language Annals, 16.* New York: ACTFL.

Moran, P. R. (2001). *Teaching culture: Perspectives in practice.* Scarborough: Heinle & Heinle.

Scollon, R., & Scollon, S. W. (1995). *Intercultural communication.* Oxford: Blackwell.

Seelye, N. (1988). *Teaching culture.* Linwood, Il: National Textbook Company.

Terrel, T. (1977). A natural approach to second language acquisition and learning. *Modern Language Journal 61,* 325-337.

Tomalin, B., & Stempleski, S. (1993). *Cultural awareness.* Oxford: Oxford University Press.

Chapter 16
Teaching Materials

Chapter Sixteen focuses on how to design materials, how to evaluate them, and how to adapt them to your teaching purposes. Attention is given to developing the ability to analyze the existing textbooks and revise them in accordance with what you have learned in previous chapters.

In this chapter we will consider:

(1) What are the basic steps a writer goes through in designing an English textbook?
(2) How do different types of syllabuses reflect different teaching theories?
(3) How should we evaluate teaching materials?
(4) How should we adapt materials to specific teaching purposes?

Task 1: Reflect

- Compare these two teachers who have different views on teaching materials. Which view do you prefer? Why?

1. **Teacher A** focuses on the textbook. He/She often says, "My teaching objective is "finishing Unit 2," or "doing the first ten pages." He is acting as a servant of the textbook (Cunningsworth, 1984).

2. **Teacher B** is different from Teacher A. He has defined his objectives. He searches and uses teaching materials which will help in achieving these objectives.

Materials Design

- In general, in order to design and publish materials (textbooks), a writer
  sets up goals →
  designs a syllabus →
  designs and publishes materials.

- Without doubt, the process of designing materials for the study of a foreign language is influenced by the writer's:

  (1) view of the nature of language,
  (2) view of the learner and language learning,
  (3) view of the teacher and language teaching,
  (4) perception of the whole context including the learner, teacher, and educational setting (Stern, 1983).

- Let's take a brief look at the relationship between materials design and language teaching methods. The design of materials is subject to theories of language and language learning. The relationship between theories and design will be clearer if we look at the framework suggested by Richard and Rodgers (1982). These scholars set up a useful framework to describe the language teaching method. They define the method in terms of three levels: approach, design, and procedure as:

  (1) Approach: a theory of language, language learning/teaching.
  (2) Design: the selection and description of language items, description of the role of teacher, learner, and teaching materials.
  (3) Procedure: the description of techniques and practices in the classroom.

- According to this model, a method includes three levels: an approach level, a design level, and a procedure level. These three levels are connected to each other as shown:

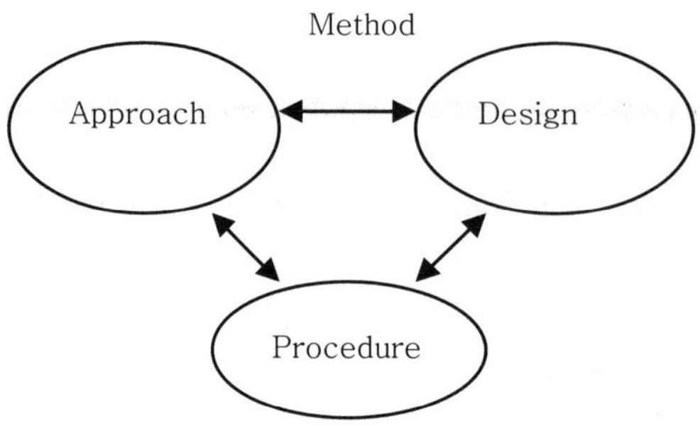

- As can be seen in this diagram, designing a syllabus and materials would fall under level two: design. It should be noted that both design and procedure are influenced by approach – the theories of language and language learning.

1. Goals

- The first step in designing materials is to define teaching goals. White (1988) distinguishes between goals, aims and objectives. Goals are very general and broad. Aims are more specific and are long-term goals. Bell (1981) calls these "key objectives." Objectives are short-term or medium-term goals. Objectives usually contain the most specific and detailed goals. In Bell's terms they are "specific objectives."

  (1) goals (general objectives) ->
  (2) aims (key objectives)->
  (3) objectives (specific objectives)

- A language program starts with a description of the overall goals, e.g., why a group of students learn English in a particular environment. These goals can be broadly stated in a national language policy, or they can be organized to address the needs of a particular group of students. Compare the following goals listed below (McDonough & Shaw, 2003, p.4). The goals in (1) and (2) are stated in terms of a national language policy, while those in (3) and (4) are stated quite narrowly.

  (1) ...to create a society that is able to utilize the language for effective communication as the need arises, and as a key to wider experiences.

For those furthering their studies, the skills learned should become an instrument used to cope with the necessity of using the language.

(2) to develop understanding of language and culture through a foreign language... to develop a positive attitude towards communication in a foreign language, and as a basic ability in practical communication through hearing and speaking

(3) ...to meet the needs of learners who need to improve their ability to communicate when socializing, telephoning, taking part in meetings...

(4) ...to help international students in English speech based universities develop the writing skills necessary for various writing projects...

- Thus we can define the goals of language teaching for a country, an age group, a whole school, a class, or an individual. The goals may have purposes such as different general educational purposes, cultural understanding, development of communication skills and so on. These goals become more specific as aims and objectives at the stage of syllabus design.

Task 2: Reflect

- Examine the teaching goals of the 7th National Elementary English Curriculum and aims/objectives of each unit of the 3rd grade English textbook.

2. Syllabus

- Once the goals are stated, the writer of a course book selects language items. A syllabus is a statement of what is to be taught and in what order. Once the goals are stated, the writer of a course book selects language items and puts them in sequence for his teaching purposes.
- There are broadly eight types of syllabuses (McDonough & Shaw, 1993). They are the result of different views of language and language learning (See Chapter 3).

(1) **Grammatical (structural) syllabus.** The grammatical syllabus is a list of grammar items, together with selected vocabulary:

Simple past
The passive
Adverbs
Conditionals

It is assumed that learning grammar will be an important factor in helping the learners learn the language. In the classroom where a textbook based on a grammatical syllabus is used, students will learn a good deal about the language, but will not be much encouraged to use this knowledge to communicate in the classroom.

(2) **Functional-notional syllabus.** The functional-notional syllabus is a list of functions (advising, greeting, introducing) and notions (the messages students will want to express, e.g. location, time, future plan). The students using the materials based on this syllabus will often learn how to use language for communication in these situations:

Making suggestions
Asking for directions
Giving advice
Introducing oneself

(3) **Situational syllabus.** The situational syllabus is a list of situations in which the students will be likely to use English. In general, a situation covers a setting (where), participants (who), and relevant objects (what). Some sample situations are:

In the restaurant
At a hotel
In the post office
At a market

(4) **Skill-based syllabus.** The skill-based syllabus is based on a list of skills that the learners will be most likely to use. Students may need a number of different skills (listening, speaking, reading, and writing), cognitive skills, study skills and composition skills (White, 1988). A

skill-based syllabus is described by combining these various skills:

Making notes from a talk
Reading for information
Using a dictionary
Writing an exam paper

(5) **Topic-based syllabus.** The topic-based syllabus is a list of topics that will be of great use to students. Example topics are:

Space travel
Animals
The weather
Smoking

(6) **Task-based syllabus.** The task-based syllabus is a list of tasks which the learners will be likely to meet outside the classroom. Here is an example.

Task: Interviews

- Language focus: question forms
- Vocabulary: meeting people
- Skills: speaking, reading, listening

(7) **Two-layered syllabus:** Most syllabuses are based on a combination of two or more different types of syllabuses. A two-layered syllabus (e.g., functions and structures) is very common. In this type of syllabus, functions are the primary organizing principle and structures are the secondary organizing principle. Here are examples.

At the bank: question forms
At a garage: imperatives
In a class: present tense

(8) **Multi-layered syllabus:** Recently course books have tended to include two or more organization principles (e.g., function, structures, skills, topics, situations). Look at the following table of contents. In the course book, the writer considers six categories of language learning

as:

① **Grammar**. Wh-questions, e.g., What...? How old...? Yes/No questions, e.g., Does he like blue?
② **Phonology**. /z/ consonant in *does/doesn't*
③ **Functions**. Asking for and giving information about name/age/likes, e.g., What's his/her name? How old is he/she? Does he/she like red? Yes, he.she does.
④ **Topics**. People's names, ages, likes
⑤ **Vocabulary**. Colors, e.g., red, blue, yellow, orange
⑥ **Skills**. Speaking/listening (exchange information, turn-taking with partner), writing (write notes including name/age/favorite color)

As can be seen in this table of contents, the writer of the material has considered several different categories related to meaning (functions, topics), formal categories (grammar, phonology, vocabulary) and skill categories (speaking, listening, and writing) at the same time. Thus six organizing principles are in play in this textbook, and they are connected to each other in a systematic way. This reflects a complex view of materials design.

Task 3: Reflect

1. Choose a unit from the 6th grade English textbook. Describe it using the terms below.

   (1) Functions
   (2) Topics
   (3) Situations
   (4) Grammar
   (5) Vocabulary
   (6) Pronunciation
   (7) Skills
   (8) Other

2. Plan a lesson for the above unit.

3. Evaluating Materials

- Compare these two teachers who evaluate materials in different ways. Which method do you prefer? Why?

  (1) Teacher A uses a course book with her students for two weeks before officially adopting it.
  (2) Teacher B has a conference with her colleagues including native speakers and they evaluate the course books together.

- No textbook is perfect. Often we have to evaluate a number of textbooks and select one for teaching. What guidelines can be used to evaluate language-teaching materials? McDonough & Shaw (1993) suggest criteria to be used in two stages: an external evaluation stage (an overview of cover, introduction, table of contents), and an internal evaluation stage (detailed examination of materials).

- The list for an external evaluation:

  (1) **Intended audience.** First you need to make sure whom the materials are for. The topics good for adults may not be suitable for children.
  (2) **Proficiency level.** Most materials state the particular level at which they aim. You should investigate whether they aim at that level successfully.
  (3) **Units and lessons.** Materials have a number of units/lessons and a suggested length of time to cover that material. You should make sure that the materials have enough units for your total class hours.
  (4) **Author's view on language and methodology.** Materials reflect the writer's view on language and language teaching. The materials reflecting recent theories and methodologies might be better.
  (5) **Visual materials.** It is worth examining whether the visual materials (photographs, pictures, charts, diagrams) are used effectively and serve any learning purpose.
  (6) **Layout.** Some textbooks have a good layout, but poor items to teach. The layout of materials should be examined in connection with the language items provided.

(7) **Tests.** Teachers need diagnostic, progressive, and achievement tests for their learners. It is worth examining the set of tests accompanying the textbook in advance.
(8) **Others.** You should also examine a teacher's book, a vocabulary list, an index of grammar items, functions and recorded materials.

- The list for an internal evaluation (Cunningsworth, 1984; McDonough & Shaw, 1993):

(1) **Language content.** This includes functions, communicative interactions, grammar, phonology, vocabulary, and skills.
(2) **Grading and recycling.** Materials can be graded in a deep, shallow, "middle of the road" manner. You have to investigate the grading of a book to see that it suits your learners. Recycled grammar items and vocabulary can facilitate learning. Recycling means a new item presented is reviewed repeatedly in the units that follow.
(3) **Presentation and practice of new language items.** This includes the significance of the presentation of new structures, and to what extent these items are related to what has been previously learned.
(4) **Developing language skills.** This includes to what extent the learning activities facilitate free production of spoken English, in what proportion the four language skills are used, and how the basic skills are integrated in activities.

4. Adapting Materials

- A decision to adopt a textbook is an initial step. But it does not mean that no further action needs to be taken after adopting the materials. In most teaching contexts, some changes need to be made even if the materials have been designed remarkably well.
- McDonough & Shaw (1993) provide reasons for adapting materials. These include:

(1) Not enough grammar coverage.
(2) Not enough practice on grammar points.
(3) Reading passages contain too much new vocabulary.
(4) Not enough guidance on pronunciation.

(5) Subjects are inappropriate for learners.
(6) Amount of material is too much or too little to cover in the given time.
(7) Dialogues are too boring and formal.
(8) Too much or too little variety in the activities.
(9) Accompanying test needed.

- These are the techniques teachers use frequently in adapting materials:

  - **Adding.** Addition implies that existing materials are supplemented by putting more items into them. There are two ways to add a new item, **extending** and **expanding**. **Adding by extending** is to supply more activities of the same type. It is called quantitative addition. Extending means that new exercises are added *within* the structure of the original materials. For example, when students need more practice on a new grammar point, the teacher may give more exercises focused on the grammar point. **Adding by expanding** is to supply more learning activities *outside* the framework of the material. It is called qualitative addition. Expansion is different from extension in that it develops the material in new directions, for instance, by adding a different language skill or a new task. As expansion of reading, the teacher may use a reading passage in order to train the listening skill of her students.
  - **Deleting.** Deletion is opposite to addition. This technique can be used on a small scale (over a part of an exercise) or on a large scale (over a whole unit). Some examples are:

    ① The material contains exercises on the alphabet, but students have already learned the alphabet.
    ② The communicative activities are too complicated for the students to tackle.

  - **Modifying.** Modifying means an internal change in some aspect of the content of the material. It can be used at the level of the exercise, or unit. There are two techniques, **rewriting** and **restructuring**. **Rewriting** changes the material and makes it more closely related to the learners' needs. Some examples are:

    ① A text may not place sufficient emphasis on listening, and the teacher feels that more material is required. The teacher can rewrite a reading passage and deliver it orally to the students.

② A text may have material that is inappropriate for the students culturally. For example, a story about a Japanese family, with Japanese names, living in a Japanese town can be modified easily by making a number of surface changes.
③ Some of the end-of-unit comprehension questions are too difficult for students. The teacher can modify them while considering the language level of students.

- **Restructuring.** Restructuring is the technique of changing the structure of the class so that the learners can participate in activities more effectively. For example, when a text contains roleplay activities for a small group, the teacher will have to divide the students into small groups and assign a role to each student.
- **Simplifying.** This technique is often applied to reading passages. The emphasis is on changing the material to match the text to the proficiency level of learners. We can often simplify a text in these terms:

① **Sentence structure.** Sentence length is reduced, or a complex sentence rewritten as a number of simple ones.
② **Lexical content.** The number of new words is controlled.
③ **Grammatical structures.** Simple grammatical structures are used. For example, passives are changed into actives; simple past into simple present; indirect speech into direct speech.

- **Reordering.** This technique puts the parts of a text in a different order. This may mean changing the sequence of the presentation of a unit, or taking units in a different sequence from that originally organized.

Task 4: Application

1. Simplify this passage.

   Once upon a time, there was a boy who lived in an African village with his father and his mother and his brothers and his sisters. The boy wanted to go hunting with his father. But his father said, "You cannot go hunting until you have a spear of your own. You must stay here and herd the sheep and milk the old white cow."

2. Choose a unit from an elementary English textbook. Decide on any features of the material you would like to change. Referring to the techniques we have been discussing, draw up some suggestions for how to adapting the material.

3. Plan a lesson based on your adaptation.

Summary

In this chapter, we have considered:

- ***Materials design.*** In designing materials, the writer first defines his teaching goals, selects language items and uses them for his teaching goals. A syllabus is a statement of what is to be taught and in what order. There are several different types of syllabuses. They are grammatical syllabus, functional-notional syllabus, situational syllabus, skill-based syllabus, topic-based syllabus, and task-based syllabus.
- ***Evaluating materials.*** When we evaluate teaching materials, we need to consider: intended audience, proficiency level, units, author's view on language and language teaching, visual materials, layout, and tests. We also need to consider: language content, grading, lesson organization, and students' developing language skills.
- ***Adapting materials.*** In adapting materials, we need to use these

techniques: adding, deleting, modifying, restructuring, simplifying and reordering.

Useful Internet Sites

1. http://eleaston.com
2. http://www.eslcafe.com
3. http://www.eslsite.com
4. http://www.geocities.com/Athens/Delphi/1979/games.html
5. http://www.eslmonkeys.com/teacher/teaching_materials.php

References and Additional Resources

Byrne, D. (1983). *Teaching oral English.* London: Longman.

Cunningsworth, A. (1984). *Evaluating and selecting ELT materials.* Oxford: Heinemann.

Moon, J. (2000). *Children learning English.* Oxford: Macmillian/Heinemann.

McDonough, J., & Shaw, C. (2003). *Materials and methods in ELT.* Oxford: Blackwell Publishing.

Nunan, D. (1999). *Second language teaching and learning.* Boston: Heinle & Heinle Publishers.

Richards, J., & Rodgers, T. (1982). Method: Approaches, design, procedure. *TESOL Quarterly, 16(2),* 153-68.

Stern, H. H. (1983). *Fundamental concepts of language teaching.* Oxford: Oxford University Press.

White, R. (1988). *The ELT curriculum: Design, innovation and management.* Oxford: Basil Blackwell.

Chapter 17
Testing

Chapter Seventeen provides general information about testing. It has two parts, the theoretical part and the practical part. In the theoretical part, testing purposes, test types, and procedures for designing a test are introduced. In the practical part, sample test items and the techniques of testing in the four language skill areas are presented.

In this chapter, we will consider:
(1) Definition of a test
(2) Discrete-point tests and integrative tests
(3) Types of tests
(4) Steps in test construction
(5) Tests for listening, speaking, reading, and writing
(6) Alternative tests

What Is a Test?

- A test, according to Brown (2004), is a method of measuring a person's ability, knowledge, or performance in a given domain. In this case "method" means a set of techniques and procedures that make a test explicit and structured. Thus a well-designed test could accurately measure a test-taker's ability within a particular domain such as listening, speaking, reading, writing, or a general ability to communicate in a given language.

Two Types of Language Testing

- Language testing trends and practices have followed the change of teaching methodology. In the 1950s, an era of behaviorism and audio-lingual teaching methods, testing focused on specific language components such as phonology, grammar and vocabulary. Hence discrete-point tests were generally favored. In the 1970s and 1980s, an era of communicative language teaching, an integrative view of testing was popular. During this period, the general competence of the test-taker was the focus in language testing.

1. Discrete-Point Tests

- In the 1950s and 1960s, discrete-point tests were used frequently in language classrooms. The assumptions underlying the tests were:

  (1) language can be broken down into its component parts;
  (2) the component parts can be successfully tested in isolation.

- The major component parts were:

  (1) the skills of language such as listening, speaking, reading, and writing;
  (2) the components of language such as phonology, lexicon, grammar, and discourse.

- This is Harris's (1969) chart of skills and components based on a discrete-point view of language.

Components	Language Skills			
	Listening	Speaking	Reading	Writing
Phonology/orthography				
Structure				
Vocabulary				
Rate and general fluency				

- Sample discrete-point test items are:

> *(Multiple-choice phonology test)*
> Circle "S" for same or "D" for different.
> 1. (led let) S D
> 2. (bit bit) S D
> 3. (seat set) S D
> 4. (too to) S D

> *(Multiple-choice vocabulary test)*
> 1. He's not married. He's ___________.
>   A. young
>   B. single
>   C. first
> 2. If there's no doorbell, please ___________ on the door.
>   A. type
>   B. knock
>   C. shout

2. Integrative Tests

- In the 1970s and 1980s, scholars argued that language competence is a set of abilities that cannot be tested separately. They argued that vocabulary, grammar, phonology, the four language skills and other discrete elements of language could not be separated from each other in language performance. They went on to claim that discrete-point tests could not capture the test-taker's language competence successfully. They suggested integrative tests instead, claiming that the whole is better than the sum.
- Cloze tests and dictations are good examples of integrative tests. A cloze test is a passage to be read in which every 6th or 7th word has been deleted. The test taker is asked to write the words that fit in those blanks. Look at the sample cloze test below. Notice it starts and ends with full sentences.

(Students fill in the blanks)
The itsy bitsy spider climbed up the waterspout. Down came the rain and (1)___ the spider out. Out came (2)____ sun and dried up all (3)____ rain. And the itsy bitsy (4)____ climbed up the spout again. The itsy bitsy spider climbed up the kitchen wall.
(Possible answers: washed, the, the, spider)

- In dictation, learners listen to a passage read by a teacher and write what they hear, using their short term memory
- . Dictation generally has three stages:

(1) a first reading at normal speed,
(2) a second reading with a long pause after each phrase (to give the learner time to write down what is heard),
(3) a third reading at normal speed (to give the learner a chance to check what they wrote).

Why Do We Test?

- There are many reasons why we give tests. We give tests to our students to encourage them, to check their progress, or to find out their learning difficulties. Those different testing purposes demand different types of tests. Heaton (1990) has provided the following types of tests and their purposes.

1. Finding out about progress (progress tests)

- Perhaps the most important reason for giving tests is to find out how well the students have learned the skills and information which have been taught. Tests for this purpose are called progress tests.
- Progress tests usually produce high marks (80 or 90 per cent). If we test what has been taught and practiced, then we should expect students to score fairly high marks. If most of the students fail to score high marks, something must have been wrong with the teaching or textbook.
- Giving progress tests regularly is very helpful. It helps teachers focus on certain language skills, elements, and teaching points. It may also prevent

us from hurrying on to finish a unit or a textbook before the students are ready.

- However, over-testing should be avoided. Too many tests can have harmful effects on students' attitudes toward learning. Also informal tests are less stressful than formal tests. The best test is one which students see as an enjoyable and meaningful activity.

2. Encouraging students

- Another important reason for giving tests is to encourage students. Learning English is different from learning science and math. In these latter subjects, students can see their progress by asking themselves what they have learned. However, this is not the case when learning English. It is often difficult for students to see their own progress. Most students make slow and steady progress when learning a language.
- When children start to learn English, they have a great deal of interest and appear to make good progress. They are filled with enthusiasm. Later, however, when they find it difficult to see their progress, they lose their initial enthusiasm. In fact, they are making steady progress all the time. The problem is that the progress is so slow that they simply cannot see it.
- A classroom test can help to show students the progress which they are making. It shows them the learning goals which they have reached. It could help students keep their initial enthusiasm.

3. Finding out about learning difficulties (diagnostic tests)

- Doctors diagnose illness in order to cure their patients. Similarly teachers diagnose problems in order to teach effectively. A good diagnostic test helps teachers to find their students' problems and difficulties. When teachers locate their students' difficulties, they can then plan appropriate remedial teaching programs. Here is an example of a diagnostic test.

(A sample grammar test)
1. See you tomorrow at six. (0)
2. There is a zoo beside the park (0)
3. Sue and Ann lives here. (x)
4. David live in a small village. (x)
5. Do you like dogs? (0)

(Diagnosis)
Prepositions: no problems
Verbs: problems with present tense

4. Finding out about achievement (achievement tests)

- In certain ways an achievement test is like a progress test. It measures what has been taught. But it is usually designed to cover a longer period of learning than a progress test. It is often given at the end of a school year or at the end of a semester in the form of a formal examination.
- When done correctly, an achievement test measures a student's mastery of what has been taught. It covers a suitable selection of the contents of a syllabus or a course book.

5. Placing students (placement tests)

- The purpose of a placement test is to sort students into groups according to their language ability. Thus placement tests are used to find out students' current level of competence and to place them in a specific course or level. There are various types of placement tests: for example, fill in the blanks, dictation, composition, or oral interview.

6. Selecting students (selection tests)

- A selection test is used when there are far more candidates than the number of places available. The purpose of this test is to compare the performances of the students and select only the best. Selection tests are usually set by outside specialists such as the Ministry of Education or public examining bodies.

- Selection tests are norm-referenced. We use a selection test to compare a student's performance with the performance of the other students in the same group. For example, is the student in the top 20% of the group? Is he/she in the bottom 10% of the group?

7. Finding out about proficiency (proficiency tests)

- The purpose of a proficiency test is to measure how well students perform a certain task. Most proficiency tests focus on assessing the students' ability to use English in the area of science, medicine, social studies, or technology.
- Proficiency tests are criterion-referenced. We use a criterion-based test to find out whether a student can perform a certain task or not. For example, can the student write a letter asking for information about something? Can the student read books about social science at the college level?

> ♦ **Norm-referenced and criterion-referenced tests:** Norm-referenced tests focus on how well a student performs when compared with the other students in a group; while criterion-referenced tests focus on how well a student performs a certain task and are designed to give test-takers feedback on a specific course or lesson objectives.

Task 1: Reflect

(1) Suppose you have a group of new students who appear to have different levels of English competence. As an English teacher what are you going to do about this?

(2) Look at the 7th National English Curriculum, and find out about the guidelines for testing.

Steps in Test Construction

- In general, teachers do not design selection tests or proficiency tests. Teachers use the tests constructed by specialists. However, they may have many chances to design placement, progress, or achievement tests. Here are some practical steps in designing classroom tests suggested by Brown (2004).

1. Determine Testing Objectives

1) The first step toward designing a test is to determine and state clear and appropriate objectives.
2) In order to determine objectives, you need to decide what it is you want to test. Perhaps you will have to take a careful look at everything the students should know, or examine the objectives for the unit you are teaching.
3) Objectives should be stated in terms of clear performance so that you can test them. An objective that states, "Students will learn sentences in the past tense" is not testable. It is not in performance terms. So you don't know whether students should be able to understand the sentences in spoken or written English. But the objective "Students will recognize and produce sentences in the past tense in simple conversations with correct pronunciation of the past tense verbs" is stated quite clearly.

2. Draw up Test Specifications

- The next step is to draw up test specs (specifications) for your classroom use based on your objectives. Your test specifications can include (a) an outline of the test, (b) skills, (c) item types and tasks. Example test specs are:

(Test specs)
Speaking (5minutes per person)
Format: oral interview, T and S
Task: T asks questions (5 questions total)
Listening (10 minutes)
Format: T makes audiotapes
Task: multiple-choice items (10 items total)
Reading (10 minutes)
Format: cloze test items
Task: fill-in-the-blanks (10 blanks total)

3. Devise Test Tasks

- Now you are ready to draft test items based on your test specs. For example, you draft questions for your oral interview as seen in the oral interview format below. You begin and end with nonscored items (warm-up and wind-down). Those items are designed to set students at ease. Level-check questions are intended to test your testing objectives, and probe questions (questions out of objectives) are designed to test the student's oral ability a little beyond the testing objectives.

(Oral interview format)
A. Warm-up: questions and comments
B. Level-check questions
  1. Tell me what you did last weekend.
  2. Tell me about a trip you took last year.
C. Probe
  1. What do you think about ______?
  2. How do you feel about ________?
D. Wind-down: comments and reassurance

- In drafting and revising test items, you will ask yourself these questions:

(1) Are the directions clear?
(2) Is there an example item to introduce each section?
(3) Does each item measure a specified objective?
(4) Is each item stated in clear, simple language?

(5) Is the difficulty of each item appropriate?
(6) Does the sum of the items reflect the learning objectives?

4. Design Multiple-Choice Test Items

- Multiple-choice items seem to be the simplest kind of questions to construct. But they are difficult to design correctly (Brown, 2004, p.55). These four guidelines are useful for designing multiple-choice items (Gronlund, 1998; Brown, 1996):

(1) Design each item to measure a specific objective.
(2) State both the stem and the options as simply and directly as possible. A multiple-choice item has a stem and several options to choose from as seen in the example below.

(Stem and options) S hears: Did John watch TV last night? **(stem)** S reads: A. Yes, he did. **(options)** B. Because he was tired. C. At eight o'clock.

(3) Make certain that the intended answer is clearly the only correct one.
(4) When designing items, use item indexes to accept, discard, or revise items. The item indexes are: item difficulty, item differentiation and distractor efficiency.
(5) Item difficulty (ID) is the extent to which an item is easy or difficult for the group of test-takers. ID reflects "how many students answered the item correctly."

$$ID = \frac{\text{\# of Ss answering the item correctly}}{\text{Total \# of Ss taking the test}}$$

(6) Item differentiation is the extent to which an item differentiates between high-ability students and low-ability students. An item on which high-ability students and low-ability students perform equally well would have poor item differentiation.
(7) Distractor efficiency is the extent to which the distractors (wrong answers) attract test-takers. If a distractor does not attract any

student, it has poor distractor efficiency.

Listening Tests

- There are three simple ways to test the listening skills of beginning learners: native-language responses, listening with picture cues, listening with simple task responses (Madsen, 1983).

(1) Native language responses

- Students listen to test items in English and respond in their native language. For example, you could use true-false questions with the true-false options printed in the native language.

Horses fly. *(Ss hear or read)* 맞다 틀리다 Horses are bigger than people. *(Ss hear or read)* 맞다 틀리다

How far is it to Seoul? *(Ss hear or read)* A. 아니오, 멀지 않습니다. B. 남쪽입니다. C. 약 200km입니다.

(2) Picture cues

- Visuals are often used to test listening comprehension. This technique is very useful with beginners, because they can respond even if they can't read English. The picture may have several things going on. True-false or yes-no questions can be given.

1. A girl is on the slide. True False 2. Two children are on the seesaw. True False 3. Is it raining? Yes No 4. Are these children in a park? Yes No

(3) **Task or activity responses**

- Task or activity responses can be used individually or in a group. For example, students listen to the following and act individually or in a group.

> *(Students hear and act)*
> Stand up. Walk to the door. Turn on the light. Go back to your seat. Sit down.

> *(Students hear and draw)*
> Draw a square in the middle of your paper. Make each side 5 centimeters long. Now draw another square to the right of the first square.

Speaking Tests

- Teachers can test the speaking skill of young students through directed responses, questions about pictures, reading aloud, and guided role plays.

(1) Directed response

- Directed responses are close to imitation. Examples are:

1. T: Tell me you went home.
   S: I went home.
2. T: Tell me you speak English.
   S: I speak English.
3. T: Ask her what time it is.
   S: What time is it?

(2) Picture cues

- Teachers can use pictures and objects to test the speaking skill of young children. One approach is to use simple drawings like the one below.

Tell me about this picture. What's happening here?

(3) Reading aloud

- Testing students by having them read something aloud has several advantages:

① Students all respond in the same way, so we can compare them quite easily.
② Tests of this kind are very easy to prepare and to administer.
③ We can check how well students have mastered sound-symbol relationships as they read English.
④ Reading aloud can provide some help in checking fluency.
⑤ Reading aloud can give us some idea how well our students have mastered grammar. Errors in reading aloud reflect confusion about the structure of English.

- There are two types of reading aloud tests. One type is a groups of sentences unrelated to each other. The sentences in this type of reading activity should reflect the specific points being tested.

He said he would come? [intonation] I'm the <u>sixth</u> child in my family. [consonant clusters]

- The other type is a passage of connected sentences. The material for this type can be taken from a reader.

Friday is report card day. Robin is a big kid in grade five. She gets grades for her subjects. Joe is a big kid in grade three. He gets a comment on each subject. Ben is a little kid in pre-school. There are no subjects in pre-school. There are no report cards in pre-school. Dad and Mom are happy that Robin and Joe have learned so many new things.

(4) Guided roleplay

- In a guided role play, the teacher or volunteer helper takes a fixed role, and the student responds. Usually the situation is explained before the role-play begins. Here is an example:

You are a customer in a shop. You are buying a cap. I will be the shopkeeper. T: Can I help you? S: Yes. I want to buy a cap. T: I see. Here are the caps. Which one do you like? S: I like the green one. T: Here it is. Try it on. S: Okay. How do I look? T: You look great!

Scoring

- The scoring scale for speaking is adapted from Madsen (1983):

5 points: Uses English with few errors.
4 points: Uses good English with a few errors. The errors do not make meaning obscure.
3 points: Uses fair English with several errors. The errors make meaning obscure occasionally.
2 points: Uses poor English with lots of errors. The errors often make meaning obscure.
1 point: Uses English with lots of error. The speaker is difficult to understand.
0 point: Uses English full of errors. The speaker is unintelligible.

- Brown (2004) suggested this scoring scale:

2: comprehensible; acceptable grammar
1: comprehensible; partially correct grammar
0: incomprehensible; seriously incorrect grammar

Reading Tests

(1) Picture cues

- Multiple pictures can be used. Students read a sentence and circle the right picture.

The children are riding their new tricycle.

- Using a picture cue, multiple-choice or yes-no questions can be asked:

> 1. The robber steals things because ___
>   A. it is dark.
>   B. the family is at home.
>   C. the family does not hear him.
> 2. Is the boy watching TV?　Yes　No
>
> 

(2) **Phrase and sentence cues**

- The true-false sentence is often used with beginners.

> 1. The sun sets in the east.　T　F
> 2. The sun is smaller than the moon.　T　F

- The true-false sentence can be changed into a multiple-choice type:

> 1. The sun sets in the _______
>   A. east　B. west　C. north　D. south
> 2. The sun is smaller than _____.
>   A. the moon　B. the earth　C. the sea　D. the universe

(3) **Multiple-choice cloze**

- Cloze tests may be too difficult for young children. Multiple-choice cloze tests are less difficult for beginning students.

Annie is an apple farmer. (She, He, They) has a big orchard of (pear, apple, orange) trees. In the fall she (cooks, buys, picks) baskets of round, (ripe, blue, white) apples. She grows many kinds (at, of, on) apples. She sorts and organizes them for sale. *(Answers: She, apple, picks, ripe, of)*

Writing Tests

(1) **Multiple-choice spelling task**

- Students choose the word with the correct spelling and write it in the space.

1. He washed his hands with ______ A. soap B. sope C. sop D. soup 2. When I went to the door, no one was ______ A. their B. there C. they're D. thair

(2) **Changing phonetic symbols**

- Students read words in which a letter or letters are written in a phonetic symbol. They write the words using the regular alphabet.

1. tea /ʧ/er ______________[teacher] 2. /ð/ is______________[this] 3. n /au/______________[now]

(3) Sentence combining

- Students combine sentences by adding a connective.

> 1. He likes ice cream _____ he does not like milk. (but)
> 2. He likes to swim _____ he goes to a swimming pool. (so)

- Advanced students can be asked to combine sentences by changing them.

> He is hungry. He wants to buy pizza.
> He wants ______________________________
>
> *(Answer: to buy pizza because he is hungry.)*

(4) Sentence expansion

- Students add words or phrases to a sentence.

> 1. The (   ) boy likes to play basketball in a (   ) park.
>   *(Possible answers: tall, large)*
> 2. His (   ) shoes surprised everyone (   ).
>
>   *(Possible answers: small, in the classroom)*

(5) Copying

- Students copy sentences using a sentence structure format.

Yesterday Last week This morning	my mom cooked a meal for	my friends. my family. us.

(6) Oral cloze

- Students have a written text with some words missing. They hear the text and fill in the missing words.

(Students hear this) An egg is an egg until it hatches. And then it is a chick. A branch is a branch until it breaks. And then it is a stick. Nothing stays the same. Everything can change. *(Students read this)* An egg is an (   ) until it hatches. And then it is a (   ). A branch is a (   ) until it breaks. And then it is a (   ). Nothing stays the same. Everything can (   ).

Alternative Tests

- Traditional standardized tests are one of many possible types of assessment. In the early 1990s, scholars realized that all people and all skills could not be measured by traditional tests. They proposed alternative tests such as performance tests, portfolios, journals, observations, self-assessments, peer-assessments, etc.

1. Performance Tests

- Every test score has a slight degree of uncertainty. Some students may not be in their best condition when taking a test. Some test questions may favor certain students over others. Also there is no such thing as a perfect test. Hence important decisions should not depend only on simple test scores (Heaton, 1990; Bailey, 1998).
- Traditional tests often cannot measure the actual performance of test-

takers. For example, if a child were asked to describe a house, to work with peers to design a house, and to explain the project to the rest of the class, traditional testing would not measure his performance. In performance tests, however, the performance of these actions can be evaluated through direct observation by a teacher, by oneself and by peers.

> ◆ Suppose that you are on an airplane. It is bound for an English-speaking country and the pilot, copilot and navigator are all nonnative speakers of English. Which of the following situations would make you happiest?
>
> (1) The flight crew members had all passed a multiple-choice test of listening comprehension about topics of general interest.
> (2) The flight crew members had all passed a face-to-face oral interview in English on general topics.
> (3) The flight crew members had all passed an authentic test of oral English communication based on recordings of actual conversations between air traffic controllers and airline pilots (Bailey, 1998).

- This situation shows what is called a performance test. O'Malley and Valdez Pierce (1996) provided these characteristics of performance tests:

  (1) Students make active responses.
  (2) They engage in higher-order thinking, with open-ended tasks.
  (3) Tasks are meaningful, engaging, and authentic.
  (4) Tasks call for the integration of language skills.
  (5) Both process and product are assessed.
  (6) Depth of a student's mastery is emphasized over breadth.

2. Portfolios

- A portfolio is a collection of student work that tells the teacher about the student's effort, progress and achievement (Brown, 2004). In making portfolio selections, the student should be an active participant. In looking over a portfolio, the student, parent, and teacher will see the student's language development as well as his/her cultural background, personality, special abilities and talents.
- Portfolios may include (Brown, 2004):

  (1) essays and compositions
  (2) reports, and project outlines
  (3) poetry and creative writing
  (4) artwork, photos, and newspaper or magazine clippings
  (5) audio and video recordings of presentations, or demonstrations
  (6) journals, diaries, and other personal reflections
  (7) tests, test scores, written homework exercises
  (8) notes on lectures
  (9) self- and peer-assessments.

Task 2: Application

1. Consider your assessment of the achievement of your students and how you will report on their progress at the end of a school year.

2. Work in groups. Select an English textbook, and design an achievement test which will be administered at the end of a semester.

Summary

- In this chapter, we have considered:

1. ***Definition of a test.*** A test is a method of measuring a person's ability, knowledge or performance in a given area (such as speaking, listening, reading, and writing) or a person's general competence.
2. ***Discrete-point tests and integrative tests.*** The assumption made in the use of discrete-point tests is that language competence can be broken down into a set of component parts. Discrete-point tests focus separately on vocabulary, grammar, phonology, and each of the four language skills. In integrative tests, however, the assumption is that language competence is a set of abilities that cannot be tested separately. Hence they measure the competence of a test-taker in integrative ways, by using dictation and/or cloze tests, etc.
3. ***Test types.*** The major test types are progress tests, diagnostic tests, achievement tests, placement tests, selection tests, and proficiency tests. They have different testing purposes. For example, the purpose of progress tests is to find out how well the students have learned the skills and areas which have been taught; while the purpose of diagnostic tests is to find out the learning problems and difficulties of students in order to teach effectively.
4. ***Steps in test construction.*** When we design a test, we go through a set of steps. We determine testing objectives, draw up test specifications, devise test tasks, and design multiple-choice test items.
5. ***Sample test items for each of the four skills are:*** native language responses, picture cues, task or activity responses for listening tests; directed responses, picture cues, reading aloud, guided role plays for speaking tests; picture cues, phrase/sentence cues, multiple-choice cloze for reading tests; sentence combining, sentence expansion, copying, and oral cloze for writing.
6. ***Alternative tests.*** In addition to the traditional tests listed above, there are several types of alternative tests such as performance tests, portfolios, journals, self-assessments, peer-assessments, and observations.

Useful Internet Sites

- http://www.btinternet.com/~ted.power/esl0704.html

References and Additional Resources

Heaton, J. B. (1990). *Classroom testing*. London: Longman.

Bailey, K. M. (1998). *Learning about language assessment*. New York: Heinle & Heinle Publishers.

Brown, H. D. (2004). *Language assessment: Principles and classroom practices*. London: Longman.

Brown, H. D. (1996). *Testing in language programs*. NJ: Prentice Hall Regents.

Gronlund, N. E. (1998). *Assessment of student achievement*. Boston: Allyn and Bacon.

Harris, D. P. (1969). *Testing English as a second language*. New York: McGraw-Hill Book Company.

Madsen, H. S. (1983). *Techniques in testing*. Oxford: Oxford University Press.

O'Malley, J. M., & Valdez Pierce, L. (1996). *Authentic assessment for English language learners: A handbook for teachers*. Alexandria, VA: Teachers of English to Speakers of Other Languages.

A COURSE FOR ELEMENTARY ENGLISH TEACHER EDUCATION

A practical guide to teaching English to children in English

▶2008년 2월 제4판 인쇄 · 발행
▶2011년 2월 제5판 2쇄 · 발행
▶2012년 2월 제5판 인쇄 · 발행
▶2013년 2월 제6판 인쇄 · 발행
▶2014년 2월 제7판 인쇄 · 발행
▶2017년 8월 제7판 3쇄 · 발행
▶2022년 2월 제7판 5쇄 · 발행
▶2024년 3월 제7판 6쇄 · 발행

연구(1차) : 김재혁(책임), 김영숙, 선규수, 오마리아, 박선호, 조경숙, 조영임
연구(2차) : 나기연(책임), 강후동, 김영민, 김재혁, 노경희, 오마리아, 우길주, 이승복
이혜경, 정영숙, 조경숙, 최희경, 홍경선
집 필 : 김재혁, 김영숙, 선규수, 오마리아, 박선호
영어교정 : Carol Moyer, David Phelps

저 자 : 김재혁, 김영숙, 선규수, 오마리아, 박선호

발 행 처 도서출판 지성계
등록번호 제 05-04-0144
주 소 광주광역시 동구 문화전당로 23번길 5-16 2F
전 화 062) 514-7530

I S B N 978-89-6103-269-8 93370

가격 : 22,000